Remote Working

Remote Working

Linking people and organizations

David Nickson and Suzy Siddons

ELSEVIER

BUTTERWORTH
HEINEMANN

AMSTERDAM BOSTON HEIDELBERG LONDON NEW YORK OXFORD
PARIS SAN DIEGO SAN FRANCISCO SINGAPORE SYDNEY TOKYO

Elsevier Butterworth-Heinemann
Linacre House, Jordan Hill, Oxford OX2 8DP
200 Wheeler Road, Burlington, MA 01803

First published 2004

British Library Cataloguing in Publication Data
Nickson, David
   Remote working: linking people and organizations
   1. Telecommuting 2. Supervision of employees 3. Personnel management
   I. Title II. Siddons, Suzy, 1942–
   658.3'12

Library of Congress Cataloguing in Publication Data
A catalogue record for this book is available from the Library of Congress

ISBN 0 7506 5859 2

For information on all Elsevier Butterworth-Heinemann
publications visit our website at www.bh.com

Typeset by Charon Tec Pvt Ltd., Chennai, India
Printed and bound in Great Britain

Contents

Foreward   vii
Preface   ix
Acknowledgements   xi

1   Introduction   1
2   Implementing remote working   7
3   Who should be a remote worker?   21
4   Skills for managers: general management skills   31
5   Skills for managers: feedback, appraisal, control and
    development   53
6   Logistics   79
7   Technology   93
8   Personal skills for the remote worker   121
9   The home office environment   137
10 The remote worker's children, relatives and pets   163
11 Risk and remote working   175
Appendix A   Example work practices   199
Appendix B   Plain English remote working policy   205
Appendix C   Site survey form   207

Glossary   209
Bibliography and sources   211
Index   213

Foreword

A few years into my working life, I was offered promotion to head office. Up until then, I had proved myself by being very effective in busy operational roles, dealing with relentless, day-to-day pressure of work in a sales operation in a major factory. To my horror, nothing happened in my smart new office. It was deadly quiet, the phone didn't ring, I got no mail, no-one put their head around the door. I thought 'funny kind of promotion this is – there's nothing to do!' It took me several days to realise that nothing was going to happen unless I made it happen. That was the point of my new role in the first place, to identify things that needed to be done and to do them. Once I'd got the message, I never looked back. The change in mindset I acquired then helped prepare me for more senior jobs as HR Director at the London Stock Exchange and later as CEO of the Industrial Society. Even more it prepared me for managing remote workers and indeed for more recent years when I have mainly worked from home.

Those who work remotely have a very different kind of life from that of most working people today. They have little in common with people who make the same daily journey to sit at the same desk, among the same people. Instead of work being mainly about *inputs* – being there, surrounded by an established working environment, available at all times, putting in the hours – it becomes focused on *outputs*, what needs to be done and what they have managed to achieve. It requires much more awareness of resources, timescales and standards and of what other people are expecting of them. Everyone involved has to learn to be more explicit and to plan ahead. It makes remote workers more self-reliant and less likely to accept a task without making sure they really do understand what it is. They learn that feedback is crucial and they learn when to ask for help.

Managing remote workers is a challenge to managers. Assumptions and working practices need to change, in some cases drastically. The organization required by the HR function, logistics, management teams and the rest of the company is considerable. The need for a book such as this is underlined by the publication (as I was writing this foreword and after the book itself was written) of a government and TUC backed Code of Practice for Remote Workers.

Even if you are an employed home-worker, you have to act like a self-employed person, treating your employer as a client and being more focused on the task and less on the development of relationships with the people at work around you. Stripped of all the facilities and support of an office environment, you have to create your own working space and disciplines and set your own priorities. You have to re-think all your former assumptions of what 'being at work' is like and become much more flexible. And you have to get other people to re-think their assumptions and become more flexible too.

Working from home doesn't suit everyone and one way this book can help both remote workers and their managers, is to clarify that. It is also amazingly comprehensive in terms of all the things we need to organize differently in our lives to support remote working, many of which we have never had to think about before. We are in safe hands: these authors have themselves made home-working a joyful, creative liberation from commuter life and an art all of itself.

Rhiannon Chapman

Preface

When we set out to write this book we had a very rose-tinted view of remote- and home-based working. Both of us have extensive experience of home working, but as freelance workers. We saw remote working mainly in terms of the freedoms, convenience, independence and opportunities it had given us. We were sure that it could provide the same benefits, and more, for mainstream business. However, once we started researching this book it became clear that, for those in the conventional employer/employee relationship, things were not going to work out so easily.

The evidence for this came from the interviews we conducted during the research phase of writing this book. It quickly became clear that the potential pitfalls were considerable. These pitfall areas included personal skills, training, logistics, regulations, operations and security. For example, support costs for remotely located equipment, with the potential requirement for home visits for installation, maintenance and training, are typically greater than they are where staff are located on a common site. Similarly, not only are not all employees happy to work remotely, many managers do not possess the skill set, nor the inclination to work well with remote staff. Then there are issues with such things as the suitability of the remote base for operations, the potential to leave remote staff isolated and demotivated, the need to maintain security of confidential information, health and safety issues and so forth. Even where remote working was effective it seemed that this was more by good fortune than design. We became less convinced that remote working was the Holy Grail. Like teleworking, it seems always to be the coming thing, but somehow fails to arrive quite as expected.

However, it was clear that where the pitfalls had been avoided, either by chance or by design, the results were convincing. People were more productive, happier (there may just be a connection here!) and felt that they had more control over both their working and personal lives. Benefits revolved around flexible working hours and the ability to prioritize work to suit both the worker and the customer without over-directive management getting in the way. In particular those working in creative and knowledge working spheres seemed most happy with remote operations. It was interesting that organizations that had set out from the beginning to have remote working found it easier than those that were converting some or all of their workforce and management to the concept.

Another point that came out clearly from the research was that remote working is nothing new. Many in the UK will be familiar with FI (known at the time of writing as Xansa), who started out with a remote working ethos in the early 1970s. This is an organization that has gone from nearly total remote working to a mainly office-based approach – seemingly in reverse to the rest of industry. Of course remote working is much older than that – the travelling sales representative has been around for hundreds of years – they have nearly always been remote, if not itinerant workers. This implies that many of the problems that crop up when remote working has been attempted should have been solved before. Similarly the military have long had methods for operating when scattered far and wide – we were particularly impressed with the 1937 edition of the *RAF Pocket Book* (known as AP 1081), which provides an officer with everything and every process they could ever need to operate remotely. Remote working has been around for some time and there is no reason why it cannot be made to work every time.

In summary, whilst it is clear that is perfectly practical for a significant fraction of the workforce to be remote-based, if benefits are to be realized then a real investment in skills, equipment and business processes will be needed. This book identifies what has to be addressed, and suggests how to go about implementing remote working in a way that delivers real value both to the organization itself and to the people who are working remotely on that organization's behalf. What this comes down to is that, if there is a strong business case for having someone remote-based, then it will make sense to do it; if there is not, then it is a case of *caveat emptor*.

Acknowledgements

Because this book was largely research driven, there are too many people to thank individually. If you have contributed, possibly via one of the many websites we visited, and are not mentioned here please know that we are grateful for your help.

We would also like to thank: Rhiannon Chapman, Steve Roberts, Jan Carter, Dorothy Cassells, Eric Cassells, Louise Arnold, Ailsa Marks, Cherry Mill, Penny Siddons, Dr Julian Bailey.

Finally, a special mention for Sarah Gee, who provided the case study for Chapter 2 and acted as an independent reviewer.

1

Introduction

Estimates vary, as do definitions, but today there are reckoned to be over 2 million people in the UK who are either full- or part-time home workers. This may not be the much-heralded teleworking revolution forecast from the late 1970s onwards but it is a very significant minority. As such it is one that needs to be managed and supported effectively if the benefits of remote working are to be realized.

This book is aimed at all those who manage remote workers, those who are implementing remote working and, finally, remote workers themselves. The emphasis is on remote workers who are employees, but the areas relating to the skills needed to manage or work from home apply equally well to the self-employed and freelance. The goal is to enable remote workers and their managers to work effectively *together* to realize the benefits of home working.

The organizations targeted here will range from small to large and from those that may have a handful of remote workers through to those that will have thousands. Similarly, these organizations will vary from those that are almost completely office-based through to those that are virtual companies with minimal physical presence in the form of office space. Whilst dealing with these extremes it is the authors' expectation that most remote working schemes will apply to a significant minority of the workforce in a medium- to large-sized organization.

Why is Remote Working Beneficial?

The potential benefits for both the remote worker and the sponsoring organization stem from flexibility and cost-effectiveness. Examples include:

- fitting in family commitments with work
- elimination of wasted commuting time
- reduction in expensive office space
- improved work/life balance
- flexible working time
- improved geographical coverage.

Realizing these benefits cannot be taken for granted; the sponsoring organization will have to provide both the operational and organizational support needed to make them deliverable. In addition, both office- and home-based staff will need to have the right skill set in addition to the specialist skills needed to do their job. In other words, it is unreasonable to take a person out of their office desk and drop them into a cupboard under the stairs with a computer and a mobile phone and expect things to carry on as before. It may work, but it will be surprising if it does. For remote working to pay off there needs to be an investment in training and infrastructure to support it.

The case example below is from the Department of Trade and Industry (DTI) website (© Crown Copyright) and shows that remote working can deliver real benefits to both employer and employee.

The Co-operative Bank in Manchester employs teleworkers in its Managed Accounts team. By working from home, teleworkers save on office clothes, travelling time and costs. The Bank benefits from staff retention and increased productivity.

Kirsty Milne has worked for the Co-operative Bank in Manchester for some fifteen years. She lives 35 miles from the Bank's offices in Manchester and used to spend three hours a day travelling to and from work. But since 1995 she's been teleworking. It's completely changed her life and she loves it.

Are you suited to working from home?

'I applied to do telework and was given a psychometric test and interviewed to see if I'd be suited to working at home. I work a 35-hour week and I'm the team coach for all the teleworkers. I help them develop skills so they can move through the Bank if they wish.'

Work–life balance

All teleworkers are still part of the Managed Accounts team and go into the Bank once a month:

'We teleworkers are treated exactly as we would be if we were in the office. When I worked in the office, I didn't have a social life in the week and often didn't see my husband because he works in the evenings. The travel was particularly stressful.'

Home working saves money

'Now I don't feel so tired all the time. I can even walk the dogs before I start work each morning. By not travelling to Manchester I've saved money. I've sold my car, and saved on clothes for work and food. I know I'm much more productive because there are no interruptions.

'I think the Bank gains too because it retains staff. It takes two years before people are fully experienced. Training them to that point is very expensive. If they leave they take the knowledge with them. Costs for setting up employees with home workstations has been significantly lower than buying additional office space.'

Selecting the right people

The Bank is very careful how it selects people, particularly because of the potential isolation. Staff need to be highly motivated. All equipment is supplied and the Bank checks the home for health and safety. All teleworkers need a minimum of two years' experience to gain a wide knowledge of the Bank's products.

Who is a Remote Worker?

For the purposes of this book, a home or remote worker is anyone who is based at home and uses it as their main place of work at least for two days a week. Examples of remote workers include: journalists; information technology specialists; trainers; sales staff; service engineers; installation engineers; maintenance staff; telesales; graphic artists and illustrators; designers; architects; district nurses and midwives; financial advisers.

This is quite a varied list, but the one thing they will all have in common is that they do not have an office- or factory-based location from which they operate every day. Although what they do will be very different, they will all encounter problems associated with being home-based, such as space for equipment, communications with the home office, need for management support and so on. The remote worker needs skills and operational support over and above that of the on-site employee.

Why are They Different?

The main difference is that they are remote from the parent organization. They have to operate largely unsupervised and have to manage their own time and schedules. Consequently they need skills over and above those needed to do the job in a more conventional working environment. Furthermore, those they work with, those they work for, and those that work for them will need an expanded set of skills if they too are to be effective.

A consequence of this is that remote working is not for everyone, and whilst there are relatively few who are totally unsuited to any amount of remote working, many will need help and careful management support if they are to be effective and happy. This book aims to provide both employers, employed, and the self-employed with a grounding in the organizational and personal skills and support structures needed to get the best from remote working. It also intends to help identify those who would not benefit from being based at home.

Key Points

Research has shown that one of the main problems with remote based workers is that they tend to work too much rather than too little, with consequent danger of burn out.

Scope and Depth

This book is aimed at helping any organization that is looking at implementing remote working for anything up to several hundred remote workers. It is assumed that these workers may be distributed geographically but will be within one country – all examples relating to rules and regulations have been taken from the United Kingdom. Some suggestions on additional points to be considered when operating internationally are given, but only a very limited amount of research has been put into this area.

In order to cover all the areas that need to be addressed, this book deals with a number of specialist subjects. Most of these merit whole books in their own right, and the bibliography lists titles that offer in-depth material. However, in order to provide the non-specialist with the bare bones of each subject a potted introduction to each area has been provided as well as the points that are specific to remote working. It is not the intention to try to give people instant expertise in these subjects, such as security and logistics, but to provide the knowledge needed to ask the right questions of the appropriate specialist.

What's in the Book?

The book is split into broadly three parts.

The first two chapters form an introduction and overview and are for all readers. They introduce the structure of the book, the concepts behind it and what the reader will get out of it. The main concepts of the book will be presented and readers will be able to quickly find out where in the book to get help with their remote working needs.

The next group of chapters (Chapters 4–7) addresses operational and organizational considerations. This is mainly targeted at the human resources staff and managers who will have home-based staff in their organization and addresses the organizational and operational issues that will need to be covered in implementing home-based working. Chapters 4 and 5 define at some length the skills that managers will require if they are to make remote working successful for both the organization and the home-based staff, while Chapters 6 and 7 consider logistic and technological issues. These chapters will raise awareness of the responsibilities of employers for home-based staff and what they need to do to ensure the best chance of success. Although these responsibilities include complying with Health and Safety and Employment regulations, readers should note that this is not a legal textbook. Further reading is suggested for those with a need to know.

Chapters 8–10 deal with the remote worker's environment, the skills they will need and the practical issues revolving around being home-based and working successfully. Both the HR/management community and the remote workers themselves will find useful information here. Management will need to ensure that the relevant training and support exists to allow both the worker and the organization to realize the benefits of home working.

For anything that involves significant organizational change, as the implementation of remote working does, assessing the risks associated with it and taking appropriate action to contain them is highly recommended. The final chapter is therefore concerned with risk management, and proves to be a good way of summarizing all the things that need to be put in place in order for a remote working system to be successful and effective.

In summary the book provides a guide for anyone implementing remote working, whether they are employer, employee, or self-employed. Used as a checklist for what needs to be put in place, it will significantly increase the chances that all those involved – both those whose role is inside the organization and those people who are to work remotely from it – will benefit from the experience.

2

Implementing Remote Working

This chapter is a master checklist for implementing a remote working system and introduces all the concepts that are covered in detail later in the book. The objective is to communicate the scope of remote working and all the factors that need to be considered, and dealt with, if it is to be successful. There are many examples of failed remote and home working programmes, whose demise was due to overlooking the true scope of the project. It is not just a matter of giving someone a notebook computer and telling them, 'As of Monday, you work from home.'

Scope of Implementation

Figure 1 shows the high level activities that need to be considered when implementing remote working. This will be true if remote working is being considered for the first time or if roles/people are being added to an existing remote working system.

Figure 1

These activities form quite a list, and the monitoring and change element is there to make sure that it is understood that implementing remote working is an ongoing process, with associated overheads in terms of both costs and human resources. Although these are covered in greater depth in the rest of the book, a short brief of the scope of work to be expected is provided here.

Key Points

Do not underestimate the scope of any remote working implementation – even a single remote worker needs a sound infrastructure to support him or her.

Home/Remote Office

If a worker is to be wholly or partially based at home, then the location needs to be suitable for them to do so. This means that the home facilities that are to be used need to be assessed in terms of accommodation, access, ventilation and heating/cooling, physical security, suitability for installation of equipment, compliance with regulations, health and safety and tax implications. This may require a site survey and will certainly require information to be gathered from the remote worker.

The ratio between remote and office-based working will have significance here. Someone who is only working at home one day a week can get away with a more basic environment than another who is at home three or more days a week. The former may only need a table upon which to put a notebook computer and a mobile phone. The latter will need something closer to a conventional office suite.

Technology and Security

For most remote workers, though doubly so for those in knowledge working, information and communications technology will be a critical component in enabling them to do the job. They will need equipment that is both suitable for the work involved and useable in the home, or remote, environment.

Security is also a critical factor, both physical and technological. Remote workers are more at risk from both cyber and physical crime than those based at an organization site. For example, it is impractical to have security guards at every remote worker's home to protect the premises and vet visitors. Similarly, a home environment will have a wide range of visitors and trades people passing through, often outside the control of the remote worker. Teenage children can be seen as a particular risk where IT is concerned, often having more technical ability than the remote-working parent. A workable security policy needs to be developed that takes these factors into account when implementing remote working.

Related to both technology and security is business continuity. Remote workers need to be able to safeguard information and have sufficient support to allow them to keep working in the event of equipment failure. It requires more support and planning to provide this remotely than it does in a conventional office environment.

Logistics and Support

Being remotely based, even part-time, implies that there will be an additional requirement for support for remote workers. Part of this will relate to the logistics associated with people who are not based on an organization site. Additional support will be needed for mail, technical support, deliveries and collections, communications, maintenance, and meetings. There is nothing that is required that has not already been solved, for example for roving sales staff, however it is important that the logistics support is put in place before remote workers need to rely on it. A common message from those we interviewed was that it was easy to underestimate the support that remote staff would need, particularly in the early stages when there is likely to be much to learn about how processes work. It was also reported that getting these processes wrong quickly demotivated remote workers.

Key Points

Get the logistics and support right before you start remote working.

Skills

Both managers and workers will need additional skills if they are to operate within a remote-working environment. It is taken for granted that they have the skills needed to do their existing jobs (though it is always worth checking). Indeed, track record is often a consideration when assessing a person's suitability for remote working. A person who is not punctual, is disorganized or poor at time management may need a level of supervision not available to the remote worker. Similarly the greater level of trust needed in a remote worker makes a good track record important. To be successful they are likely to need improved skills in communication, time management, delegation, appraisal, leadership, self-motivation, and related areas. Some people will be more suited than others, though the majority can be effective if given any necessary additional training.

Key Points

Some people are happier working remotely than others are. It is important to keep this in mind when choosing people for remote work. For example, those who miss the social contact from office work can benefit from a mixture of remote- and office-based working, reducing the feelings of isolation that they may have.

Risk

Risk management is much overlooked and misunderstood in any project environment. This has been found to be the case with most of the remote working implementations that the authors have come into contact with. Little attempt was made to assess the risks associated with the implementation or strategies that could be used to minimize the chances of them occurring or to mitigate their impact. The main consequence of this was that problems came to light when the implementation was live, that is, when the remote workers were actually trying to do their jobs, with consequent loss of productivity and, more importantly, frustration and disillusionment with the concept as a whole. It has also meant that many issues have to be solved 'live' rather than anticipated with a contingency plan in place. It is strongly recommended that a thorough risk management exercise is undertaken as part of implementing remote working and that it is monitored throughout the life of remote working.

Suitability of the Role/Worker

Not every role is suitable for remote working – though in most cases even if the entire role is not, then part of it may be. This is further complicated by the proportion of time that a remote worker may spend away from the conventional office. For example, one organization whose policies were brought to the attention of the authors classified two roles, based upon the percentage of time spent remote working. They defined one level as being for those who spent up to 40% of their time home-based and the next level as those spending more than 40% home-based. The approval criteria applied to the higher level were stricter than those applied to the lower one. In the case of the former, the scheme was open for all their staff – anyone could apply to have their role/themselves considered for remote working. The higher percentage case was only considered if it was seen to be of significant benefit to both the organization and the employee, the rationale being based upon the higher costs involved in providing a suitable home environment and the greater skills required of both the remote worker and their management.

Similarly every manager/worker is not suitable to this way of working either. For instance, if a worker has very poor time management and organizational skills it is unlikely that remote working will pay off without suitable training. Also, as discussed in Chapter 3, the role itself may be unsuitable. Getting this right for any individual has to be done not only at the start of remote working, but re-evaluated as circumstances change.

Processes and Procedures

Most organizations will have some process and procedures in place that relate to day-to-day running and longer-term strategies and reporting. A keynote that came from the research for this book was that well-defined and effective processes were critical for the success of any medium- to large-scale implementation. The scope of the processes will need to include all the areas outlined here and be developed and tested as part of the implementation. A typical list would include health and safety, suitability of role/worker, home environment, management, risk assessment, support, absence and sickness, performance monitoring, insurance, and terms and conditions. Do not underestimate what is involved here.

Key Points

Processes and procedures for remote workers need to be easily understood and require the minimum of supporting paperwork in operation.

Monitoring and Change

Last of all, and the easiest to overlook, is change. However, monitoring the performance of a home-working implementation and keeping track of any changes in job roles, personal circumstances, organizational goals, customer requirements and technology and support issues is critical to maintaining the success of remote working.

Key Points

The areas outlined above should not be considered in isolation. Take the case of a remote worker whose skills and role are suitable but whose home base has no spare space for home working. If they move home this may be remedied, but at the same time the new location may be too remote for effective logistics support. A holistic approach must be taken to get the best implementation.

Case Study

The first part of this chapter has introduced the scope of the work to be done in implementing remote working. The second part is aimed at the person, or team, that will be responsible for the implementation and gives an idea of whom they need to talk to and the likely issues that will need to be addressed. It has been based on the experiences of Sarah G, who has actually implemented remote working from scratch in a large organization. The authors are grateful to have access to first-hand accounts of what actually happened from start to finish and the lessons learned from doing it.

Background

Sarah G works in human resources as part of a team responsible for implementing remote working for the UK arm of a large, international IT company. Her role included the definition of specific HR policies, testing them, helping to implement the programme, identifying training and ensuring that the implementation was effective. Her background at the time was that of an experienced HR professional. The implementation took place in 2001.

At the time Sarah G was HR Representative for the UK, and was responsible for health and safety in the organization. She was beginning a major audit, and as a result realized that they were not compliant with the legislation for remote- or home-based workers. Furthermore, they did not have any formal policy for remote working at all, which meant there were many inconsistencies that would require harmonizing. Sarah therefore raised this as an issue and the team suggested that she did some more research with the ultimate goal of finalizing a formal policy for UK remote workers.

Associated with this research was the risk that it could ultimately mean that they had current arrangements that were not appropriate, and that some remote/home workers might not have suitable home facilities in place. This could have costly implications, both in rectifying matters and from potential claims for compensation. Although the main drive at this point was for health and safety, the by-product was that many other issues that needed to be considered for remote workers were brought to light: for example, not hiring people as home-based workers before the organization knew whether it could support them and what to do if they are not required to work from home in the future.

As part of this, Sarah G had to liaise with any departments that would be affected by remote working. This was necessary to make sure any policies were workable. So that the management team could agree to it, it had to work for Facilities, Information Services and Finance. In addition, she had to obtain tax advice so that the parameters for home and remote workers in this area could be defined.

Overall, health and safety was seen as the biggest risk to home and remote working. This was because the consequence of not doing it right could be a claim against the organization for an injury – for Repetitive Strain Injury, for example, if the home work station was incorrectly set up. It turned out that whilst it was not a case of 'out of sight out of mind' for the home-based staff in career terms, that was the existing situation in health and safety terms. Just because no claims had been made to date did not mean they would not be in the future. Sarah needed to include this in the policies she was to develop.

Key Points

Sarah G: 'Many companies have just allowed this to evolve without feeling a need for a formal policy or any standards. This is a recipe for disaster, it is crucial to have parameters when dealing with any aspect of the employment contract, and your location of work does form part of the terms and conditions of employment. Organizations can leave themselves open to all sorts of challenges and criticisms if they fail to have a formal policy to take account of variances within an employee's terms. It is therefore better to create a policy in anticipation rather than trying to react to it at a later stage, learning by trial and error.'

Case Study

Start-up and research

The starting point for creating the policy was to research the subject. It was surprising to Sarah G how little had actually been written on this subject, especially since it had already become a steadily growing trend. (Of course, this was one of the driving forces behind the creation of this present book.) Sarah G quickly discovered that there were no definitive texts with the exception of the government guidelines and press releases from organizations promoting home working.

Sarah G found that even the limited amount of research material available was useful and she recommends that anyone undertaking such an exercise do likewise, supplemented by the material that would now be available in this book. Such research, particularly in large organizations should be conducted internally as well as externally. In some cases there will already be a policy informally or a policy that is perhaps operated at a different location/country that can be used as a starting point.

Key Points

Sarah G: 'Don't reinvent the wheel unless you really have to.'

Although the legislation relating to employment and health and safety may be different in each country, many of the basic requirements will still be the same. So, any policy that is found will be of help. Indeed, as many of the problems associated with remote working are related to skill, HR and logistics, then it is reasonable to expect to find a considerable amount of relevant material there.

[*Note*: Sarah G had spent some time researching homeworking as part of a college project whilst qualifying for CIPD. She found little information externally, and little internally within the local organization. However, she later came across a Corporate policy in the US which then formed the basis for UK policy.]

Sarah G also found that it was beneficial to contact other similar organizations to enquire how they had implemented or intended to implement remote working. For example, she found that participating in a salary survey group provided a useful source of contacts for sharing information. Others may also be interested in your results when you have completed your research and so are keen to help in return for the benefit of your experience.

Key Points

The company culture will determine the style of any policy that is written, so taking this into account at the beginning will be important. This will dictate how formal or informal your policy needs to be and how specific your definitions and processes are. However, regardless of style, the processes will need to cover the subject well enough to make sure that it is workable.

Case Study

Policy formulation

Once Sarah had conducted her research within and outside the organization, she began formulating the relevant policies. In doing this one of the lessons she learned was the best approach and sequence for formulating these policies. This is: definition; role assessment; individual; manager; initiation/request; decision making and review; site survey; support; and change.

Step 1 Definition: This is critical. It is essential to have a clear definition of who is/is not a remote worker within your organization. Sarah G found this to be the first step, as indeed did the authors; her experience is consistent with that of others who were interviewed in researching this book. Such a definition needs to include such things as:

- Can the job be done at home?
- Is the impact on the client/organization clear?
- What are the benefits expected?
- What are the predicted costs?

Step 2 Role assessment: The policy needs to define the criteria for assessing whether a role is suitable for home working and how the criteria should be applied. It is likely that there will be different criteria for different types of role and for different staff. These criteria may include such things as: tools, support and personal contact.

Step 3 Individual: For a particular role there will need to be criteria for the individual staff relating to both their technical and personal skill sets. These will vary. For example, a person who may be required to edit documents for publication on a website may be operating as a piece worker who simply receives packets of work for completion by a deadline. The only real difference from on-site workers' skills might be the ability to work unsupervised. However, someone who has to juggle a mixed workload, including client meetings, might need to have enhanced time management and communication skills. The criteria would be different.

Step 4 Manager: As with the individuals, the manager(s) will require additional skills compared to their on-site counterparts. As a minimum, they will need to have enhanced communication, delegation and tasking skills. Again, as with the individual, the required skills will vary with the nature of the role. This is particularly true if the managers are remote workers themselves.

Step 5 Initiating/requesting remote working: Whether the request for remote working comes from the worker or the organization is immaterial (although it is normally the former). This needs to be defined in terms of how this is done. For example, do you start by filling in a form, requesting a meeting with a line manager or HR, or is it promoted by an announcement asking for volunteers?

Step 6 Decision making and review: Someone (singular or plural) has to make the decision (and be available to re-evaluate it as needed) to allow remote working or not. This will vary according to the organization. Sarah G found that the prime candidates include: line management, HR, senior management, support, facilities etc. It may be a simple decision or it may involve sign off from all the interested parties. Typically some type of request form will be used that reflects the definitions and criteria that were defined in the earlier stages.

Sarah identified that these decisions were not 'once and for all' and that there is a requirement to consider reviews of the decision. This may simply be because it is good practice to consider a trial period to make sure that the arrangement works. It may also be to allow the decision to change to take into account changing organizational and personal requirements. In the latter case then further considerations include notice periods for changing to/from remote working and who has the authority to make the change.

Step 7 Site survey: In addition to establishing if the role, the skills of the individual and the manager were suitable, the remote location also needed a process to assess its usability for the remote worker. Sarah G found that it was necessary to define what the company considered a suitable home office to be. This depended on how strict the organization wished to be in setting these parameters. It was particularly critical to take account of health and safety factors here and throughout the policies. These will typically be different for different locations in an international organization, and are subject to change.

Step 8 Support: Sarah found that the support policy had not only to cover everything that was needed to do the job remotely but also had to include 'self help' packs suitable for use by the remote workers, for example, 'Frequently Asked Questions'. For this, input is required from all parts of the organization that have to support the remote workers. In Sarah's case these included:

- Those responsible for supplying any tools and equipment required;
- Facilities/logistics – supporting the individual and their working environment, for example insurance cover, deliveries and collection and so forth;
- How all other company processes, procedures and policies will link into the policy and where possible changes affecting remote workers should be highlighted – for example, delivery of post; issues of this type all need to be allowed for and documented;
- Anyone responsible for security – how the remote environment will be made secure to satisfy both the employing organization and the employee;
- Self help – this should cover aspects such as managing the manager, what to do about family and pets, and so forth; employers may wish to include these or give sources of references where individuals can find out more.

Step 9 Change: Finally, Sarah identified that having policies that actively considered change was an important success factor. She said that, 'you need to consider how changes are made, for example once a request is granted how is it followed up.'

One example relates to changes of location. Since these are usually contractual it is normal practice to grant a request in writing and require an employee to formally agree to the changes in their contract of employment. HR Information Systems will probably require updating. Payroll may also need to be informed if there is an allowance paid, for example for converting a home office. Internal support staff will need to be involved, such as Systems staff for ordering and installing equipment. Facilities staff will need to order office furniture and arrange installation. Other staff will need to be informed, the employee will need to work with the manager to communicate the change to the relevant people, such as staff and customers. This is not an exhaustive list and will vary depending upon the structure of the organization. However, each step of the process will need to be recorded in the policy and it is advisable to make the policy flexible and adaptable to any future changes or trends either in the legislation or your organization's working practices.

In addition, there needs to be a continual monitoring of how the remote-working policies and procedures are working. This drives a requirement for a change and review policy that takes this into account. For example, if a remote worker moves home then that site survey process would need to be revisited.

Summary

So a clear process or procedure for setting up remote working was required. This may be in the form of a single document, or a set of documents depending on the scope of the implementation. A complete example of the process that was produced as a result of Sarah G's work is included in Appendix A of this book.

The scope of these processes and policies will be wider than might be supposed at first sight. Sarah G's experience shows that remote working impacts, and requires support from, a wide range of departments from within an organization and will be non-trivial if it is to be done correctly and effectively.

3

Who Should be a Remote Worker?

As stated in Chapter 1, there are estimated to be over 2 million remote workers in the United Kingdom. With the working population estimated at 20 million, this is a significant minority that will cross many industry, occupational and role boundaries. The jobs that these people do vary considerably; all they have in common is that they are remote workers. The purpose of this chapter is to help define who might be, or become, a remote worker and to provide guidelines for deciding if a role is suitable for remote delivery.

Note: In this book the word organization has been chosen to represent any group wishing to implement remote working. This includes government (both local and national) departments, health services, commercial enterprises, charities, political parties, and social support groups.

Which Roles are Suited to Home Working?

It is easier to define the jobs that are not suited than it is to define those that are. By default the authors consider that all jobs are suitable for remote- or home-based working unless there are special reasons why they are not. Indeed, at least one organization researched had a stated policy that 'all employees may apply to have their role considered for home/remote-based working provided the total was not more than two days a week spent away from the main office'. Typical reasons why a person or job may not be suited to remote working are summarized below. Before setting out on the implementation of any remote working then these factors must be considered, and ruled out before committing to the change.

- **Security:** There may be state/government, commercial, or political information that is too sensitive to be risked on non-secure premises.
- **Equipment:** Equipment may be too bulky, have power requirements, be too heavy, may need to be shared by several employees, require constant maintenance, or simply be too expensive to locate at a remote user's home base.
- **Communication/contact:** If instant communications access is required for a role – for example a receptionist, an airport announcer and similar roles.
- **Insurance:** The value of equipment or information may be such that a company's insurers will not provide cover for it to be kept at the remote worker's home base.
- **Health and safety:** Employers are often responsible for the health and safety of remote workers just as they are for office- and factory-based staff. Any role that is being considered for remote working must be capable of meeting any relevant regulations.
- **Supervision:** Jobs that require constant supervision are unsuited to remote working, as, similarly, are supervisory roles.

Key Points

Keep in mind that even if a job is suitable for remote delivery, the worker concerned may not be suited to it.

Based on the above, it is clear that heavy engineering and much production work is unsuitable for remote working. It is very unlikely that it would be either cost-effective, practical or safe to install the equipment in someone's home. Modern Integrated Logistics Systems used in manufacturing would be quite unsuited to home-based working. At the other end of the scale, a knowledge worker such as a journalist or a computer programmer can perfectly well work remotely. The list below shows a spectrum of activities against their suitability for remote working.

- **Very suitable:** Writers, journalists, computer programmers, analysts, researchers, drivers, design engineers, health visitors, district nurses, creative workers.
- **Suitable:** Architects, advertising, carers, visiting medical staff, service engineers, business trainers, some managers, sales staff, cleaners, accountants, analysts.
- **Marginal:** Sales managers, line managers with remote staff.
- **Unsuitable:** Teachers, personnel, line managers requiring direct contact with staff.
- **Very unsuitable:** Heavy engineering, production line working, laboratory work, nurses, surgery and specialist medical procedures, security staff, receptionists, check-in staff, retail, banking.

Categories

It is quite possible, and indeed it is common, that many jobs will have some elements that are practical for remote working and others that are not. So remote workers can be split into three main groups – those who are full-time remote workers, those who work a mixture of office/customer and home-based working on a regular basis, and those who occasionally do so.

Full-time

Full-time remote workers are those who are based at home or on a client's site nearly all the time, perhaps spending as little as an hour a month actually at the employer's base. They also include those who are travelling from place to place. The sales representative, the subject of jokes in the old time music halls, is perhaps the classic example of the full-time remote worker. It is the view of the authors that these full-time remote workers will always be the minority of employed staff. Their support and management requirements need to be exactly right if they are to operate effectively.

Part-time

A growing percentage of all those who can be classified as remote workers come into this category. They split their time between the office, their home and customer premises in a variable mix according to the needs of the business. Part-time remote working can be both cost-effective and a major aid to improving the work–life balance. As with full-time remote workers effective support and management will be required.

Key Points

The percentage of remote-based working is often a factor used in determining whether a role is suitable as it is much easier from a management, cost and logistics point of view (and sometimes happier for the employee) if the worker is only away one or two days a week.

Occasional

The third category of remote worker is for those who perhaps take the odd day, 'working at home' in order to get away to concentrate on a particular task, for example writing a report, developing a new business plan, away from the distractions of the office environment. These people are not really remote workers and, other than any health and safety considerations, are not really different from any other staff. If all the remote workers within an organization are expected to be of this type then, usually, little needs to be done to support them.

Key Points

The level of support that remote workers need will vary with the amount of remote working they do. The occasional remote worker who just takes their laptop computer home to do a monthly report, as stated, probably needs no special support. The full-time remote worker needs a complete support infrastructure that takes their needs into account.

Initiating Remote Working

Although there are numerous reasons, most of them good, some not, for implementing remote working, the initial request can only come from one of two sources – those working for or those managing the organization.

Whoever is the initiator they should identify what the benefits will be and what they intend to achieve. This is important, there is pressure on organizations to offer a better work–life balance, indeed there is legislation that forces it, for example for parents. Consequently it is tempting for them to look at remote working as a simple solution for delivering this balance. However, as with any project, if you do not have a clear definition of what is to be achieved then there will be no means of knowing when it has been done.

An organization was setting up a quality-checking department that would draw upon senior staff from across the whole of England and Wales. The department was to be based in the South East of England and its work would involve staff spending half their time on site and half in the South East location. The staff approached did not look upon this very favourably, as it was not a permanent assignment so relocation was not desirable. However, they suggested that the role could be made remote-based with the South East location being used for essential meetings and briefings only. After all, they would be on site half the time.

The benefits to the organization were:

- *smaller, less expensive, accommodation needs at central office*
- *scheduling remote staff to visit sites in their area reduced travel costs*
- *better staff morale.*

The benefits to the staff were:

- *less time travelling so better work–life balance*
- *no need to consider disruption from relocation*
- *greater flexibility in doing the job.*

The only real cost to the organization was in the supply of suitably equipped laptop computers with remote access software. This was not a great additional expense as the staff involved were supplied with similar equipment already and would need a laptop to do the job even if based at the South East site. It is worth noting that the major benefits to the organization were financial but those to the staff related to quality of life.

The first step, once it has been decided to consider remote working, is to identify the main benefits and the main costs/disadvantages. These should be used as the basis of the decision to carry forward a remote working implementation. It should be noted that even where it costs more to employ remote workers the benefits in improved morale and work–life balance may still make it worthwhile. Indeed it may be the case that the remote worker is financially worse off, but prefers the option because it is the only way he or she can continue to work with the organization.

Where financial benefits are the prime motivation for either the organization or the worker (for example, less office space and reduced travel), then it is important that these are measurable and that they take into account all relevant factors.

Who is Suitable

The question of who is suitable for remote working is more complex than that of which roles are suitable. This question needs additionally to take into account the skills and needs of the worker, their manager and the impact that remote working may have on their work colleagues and the organization itself.

Key Points

Many managers put trust down as a major reason why they do not like remote working. To counter this reluctance, assessment of a person's track record can help allay fears.

Points to consider include the following (assuming the role is suitable for full/part-time remote working).

- **Remote worker**
  - Personal skills – communication, motivation, independence, self-discipline, assertion

- Professional skills – IT, remote access
- Costs/rewards
- Track record

- **Manager**
  - Personal skills, communication, leadership, delegation, motivation, training, appraisal, counselling
  - Professional skills, IT
  - Development requirement
  - Track record

Key Points

Over-controlling, cynical and mistrustful managers are often unsuited to manage any form of remote working and may need to be re-deployed to areas where remote working is not planned.

- **Colleagues**
  - Personal skills, communication, awareness, assertion
  - Professional skills, IT
  - Equal opportunities
  - Career development
- **Organization**
  - Support structure
  - Facilities, logistics, hot desk support, meeting rooms
  - Training facilities
  - Development requirements
  - Costs

These skills and organizational/support requirements will be discussed in greater detail in later chapters in this book. However, at this stage the important issue is to recognize that the impact of remote working extends beyond the individual concerned. Similarly, the benefits and costs also affect the whole organization, not just the individuals directly involved.

A large USA-based IT supplier developed a process that was based upon giving everyone in the organization the right to be considered for home working. This combined an assessment of the role, the person and the skills of the manager involved and home circumstances. The results of this assessment were used to determine whether the answer was a simple yes/no or was a 'maybe' based upon required extra development of the worker/manager. After such development had taken place the decision would be re-assessed. The organization also recognized that both roles and circumstances change and incorporated a periodic/ad hoc review process, which could alter the decision to meet with changing business and personal needs.

Selecting Remote Workers

Once an organization has determined its baseline for assessing who is suitable for remote working then a documented procedure needs to be developed. Table 3.1 gives a possible structure and content for such a document.

[*Note:* A sample process is offered in Appendix A of this book.]

Table 3.1   Procedure for selecting remote workers

Section	Description
Document description and introduction	What the document is for, who it is aimed at, any document control and circulation restrictions
Suitability checklist	Criteria against which roles and individuals are assessed for remote working
Assessment guidelines	Health and safety, skills, organization, home office suitability, information technology, personal skills, training
Organization policy	Policy currently in use for determining who can/cannot remote work. Terms and conditions that apply. Rules and regulations that apply to expenses and so on
Process	Description of processes that apply, for example how to request that role becomes remote-based, how performance is monitored, use of a trial period and so forth
Health and safety	Current rules and regulations that apply to remote workers
Tax issues	Tax implications for the remote workers that determine what they can and cannot claim and what the implications of this are for the remote workers and their personal situation

Summary

Remote working is not suitable for all jobs; however, it is clear that it is appropriate for a growing number of jobs and for elements of others. There are significant benefits in terms of work–life balance and reduced travelling and office expenses. There are also potential sources of significant costs, for example health and safety implementation in the home and increased support costs. All these need to be taken into account, together with the suitability of the person/role for remote working before a commitment is made.

4

Skills for Managers: General Management Skills

This chapter covers the general management skills that anyone managing remote workers will need if they are to promote a successful outcome. Of course, many of these skills will be the same as for managing staff in a conventional organization and no apology is made for covering what may be familiar ground here. However, the authors have focused on aspects that relate specifically to remote workers, and case notes and quotations have been drawn from those working in 'remote' situations.

Are there any significant differences between managing office- or workplace-based people and managing those who spend their working life away from the office or workplace? Certainly the five major management skills (planning, organizing, motivating, controlling and developing) will all be needed. However, the most successful managers of remote workers that we interviewed emphasized the following five skills:

- learning to trust
- selecting the right people for outworking
- communicating with remote staff
- motivating and giving a sense of belonging
- planning.

This chapter therefore focuses on these five management behaviours and how they need to be adapted to the needs of remote workers. In the following chapter we will deal with other management behaviours that are critical to the success of remote working, namely giving feedback, appraising, controlling and developing.

Learning to Trust

It is fairly easy to trust someone you can keep your eye on; it is much harder to trust someone who works distantly. This is particularly true of managers who basically believe that most workers need continual pressure and discipline to make them work and that without this people will shirk and perform badly. Managers with this mindset often attempt to micromanage their team and tend to be particularly fond of processes and procedures that make this easy to do. They also like to keep day-to-day decision making to themselves, only involving the team when the decision has been made, and then only to tell the team members what to do. Understandably this type of manager is not usually comfortable with remote workers.

We asked the managers we interviewed what they felt made them successful 'distant' managers in terms of their attitude to the people they managed. They came up with these comments:

'The team is full of people who are highly self motivated, they like doing a good job and are very good at what they do. I trust them to do their job well.'

'I mainly tell them what we want to achieve, then it's up to them to work out how to do it. Unless there's a very particular reason like Health and Safety Laws or legal considerations I don't interfere with them. I reckon I'm most useful to them when I champion their cause and motivate them.'

'If I didn't feel that they could do their job without being watched over then they wouldn't be happy working from home. If someone wants constant overseeing then they should be in an office. Anyway, most knowledge workers are self-running and don't like interference – I'm there to make it all run smoothly and not to "nanny" them.'

'We deliberately chose to use remote workers – we were an all woman company and knew the advantages to our staff of being able to work from home. As long as we set careful targets we had no

worries about people working without supervision. We all had high standards and expected the same from anyone who worked with us.'

The thread that ran through all their thinking was that they trusted their remote workers and believed that not only could they do the job, but that they would do a good job too.

Key Points

They saw themselves in the role of a facilitator and motivator rather than a slave driver or overseer. To them being a manager was not a power trip. They all made the point that trusting and showing clearly that you trusted your remote workers was the starting point for a successful working relationship.

Summary

This facilitative attitude to the role of the manager is a key factor in the success of their distant workers. It is impossible (not to say unwise) to try to micromanage people working away from the office. However, this does not mean that you can ignore remote workers and expect them to stay happy. No matter what their psychological make-up they will still need the support of and contact with the manager. This brings us onto the next skill required for those managing remote workers.

Selecting the Right People for Remote Working

Is there a profile that will fit the perfect remote worker? Probably not, but in the interviews we conducted with both managers and remote workers there were several factors that we found contented and successful remote workers had in common (Table 4.1).

The following is an extract from a questionnaire used by a large IT company using many remote workers:

Do you feel you are suited to homeworking?
❑ Do you have the right motivation to work remotely?
❑ Do you have good time management, planning and organizing skills?

Table 4.1 Profile of successful remote workers

Organizational skills	Decision making	Motivation	Communication skills
■ They were orderly. They liked to be organized in the way they went about their work	■ They had the confidence to make small to medium decisions without feeling it necessary to consult their manager	■ They were all self motivated – their prime motivator was doing a good job, to a very high standard; several interviewed said they gained more satisfaction from working things out for themselves than from consulting others	■ They all felt comfortable handling computers and using them to communicate with the office
■ Their time management skills were usually high	■ Although most of them were gregarious, they were also quite happy working on their own		■ Most of them had a good network of other remote workers and workers based in the company offices, which they used to keep themselves up to date with what was going on in the company
■ They were confident with IT	■ They liked taking responsibility for the contents of their working day	■ They gained great satisfaction from completing the tasks set for them	■ If they needed advice and clarification they were prepared to ask for it, indeed they were particularly good at cross questioning their managers when they were given an unclear brief
■ They really knew their job, and knew how it fitted into the company plan	■ They were particularly good at prioritization	■ They liked to over-perform	
■ It was possible for them to work without interruption for most of the day when they were at home	■ They liked problem solving	■ Most of them had either chosen the outworking option or had no worries when given the choice	■ They easily gave and responded to feedback
■ They were very task oriented and didn't procrastinate when faced with boring or irritating work			

❑ Are you self-disciplined?

❑ Will you be getting everything you need from your job being based at home? What about the social aspects, i.e. being on your own all day every day or most days?

Is your job suitable for homeworking?

❑ Does it involve 'thinking tasks' such as writing, research, programming or analysing?

❑ Can you and your manager measure productivity in terms of the number of projects or objectives completed?

❑ Can you work without constant access to corporate office off-line files or equipment?

❑ Can you work without daily face-to-face contact with other employees?

❑ Does your role require little supervision?

❑ Can you work outside the office without this having an adverse effect on the team you work with?

❑ Can you do your work without having to visit the office regularly?

Your manager will help you to make this assessment.

We then asked our interviewees if there were any factors that they felt would militate against successful remote working. The results were very interesting:

■ being forced to be a remote worker rather than choosing this as a way of working

■ lack of communication with head office

■ lack of support from head office

■ lack of knowledge of the job.

At the top of this list was whether they felt they had control over being a remote worker. The managers said that an effective and happy remote worker is someone who has chosen this way of working and the remote workers themselves said that coercion into outworking would have demotivated them.

The next most important factor mentioned, lack of communication, brings us on to the third specific skill needed.

Communicating with Remote Staff

For managers it is often hard enough to find the time to communicate regularly with their staff within the office, let alone those far away. One of the problems with having a dispersed team is the 'them and us' attitude. Team members situated in offices away from headquarters, even though they may have the support of their local colleagues, often feel that they are out of the decision making loop, away from the action and ignored and undervalued. The same goes for remote workers, but with the additional problem of the solitary nature of the way they work.

If a manager does nothing else, setting up and using clear channels of communication will make the functioning of remote workers much more successful. Time and again the remote workers we interviewed said that if problems arose there was always an element of miscommunication or lack of communication at the root of the problem.

If we look at how communication really happens there are several points to which managers of remote workers need to pay particular attention.

At the start of any communication the 'sender' (the person about to speak) works out what is to be said. Most of us at this point are more concerned with choosing the right words than thinking about whom we are going to be speaking to. We often make huge assumptions about this person. We assume that they will understand our language, we think that they have all the background information they need, we believe that they have the same interest in the subject that we do and that they have the same feelings of urgency that we do. Now while this is not the end of the world when we are speaking face-to-face (we can adjust what we are saying according to the looks of puzzlement, interest or worry on the part of the listener), it can be difficult when we're talking over the phone, or sending an electronic message. For this reason managers need to be much more structured when they are tasking remote workers or giving feedback on performance.

The next stage in the communication cycle is the actual transmission of the message. Face-to-face it is easy to see whether we are interrupting someone, but when communicating remotely we have no idea what the receiver is up to when they receive our message. For this reason it is useful to have a scheduled time of day when the remote worker knows that messages will be coming in. Scheduling time for communication is also a good discipline for managers – it ensures that we speak regularly to people who spend most of their time out of the office.

After transmission the reception phase of the communication cycle takes place. This is where the receiver responds and (hopefully) clarifies the message. Again, this is relatively easy face-to-face, but much more difficult remotely. Managers need to be very careful to summarize, check for understanding and gain feedback that the message has been fully understood.

Key Points

The first weeks of managing a remote worker should set a clear pattern for efficient two-way communication and set the precedent that communication is very welcome to the manager.

What needs to be communicated?

- **Changes:** changes to personnel (both management and teams), customers, responsibilities, locations, reporting structures, promotions, sackings, company policies, salaries pensions and perks, new kit.
- **Successes:** how the team is doing, both individually and as a group, new contracts, better ways of working, and most particularly successes on the part of remote workers.
- **Goals:** budgets, new customers, new marketing initiatives, new products.
- **Progress reporting:** regular updating *both ways.*

Motivation and Promoting a Sense of Belonging

This is probably the most important management skill needed when handling remote workers. All the motivational theories pay a great deal of attention to the personal side of work, to the interaction between workers and managers and workers and their work colleagues. Yet remote workers are expected to ply their trade without the apparent back up of a peer group or manager on hand. Let's look at some of the major motivational theories in the light of this and also in the light of the need for high self-motivation as mentioned earlier in this chapter.

Maslow's Hierarchy of Needs

In the mid-twentieth century Abraham Maslow postulated his theory of the Hierarchy of Needs. Here he states that: 'man is a wanting animal and rarely reaches a state of complete satisfaction except for a short time. As one desire is satisfied, another pops up to take its place.'

He states that for all of us there is a pyramid of needs (Figure 2) rising from the most basic physiological necessities to self-actualization where one's inner potential is realized.

In order to rise up the hierarchy, each need must be satisfied before that level can be passed. Indeed, if the ability to satisfy a particular need is significantly reduced – for example if at Level 4 esteem from others is completely lacking, the need in the level below – in this case the need for affiliation with others, will become extremely important.

So what are the basic needs that need to be supplied at level 1 for a remote worker?

- A place to work (see Chapter 9)
- The tools necessary for their work

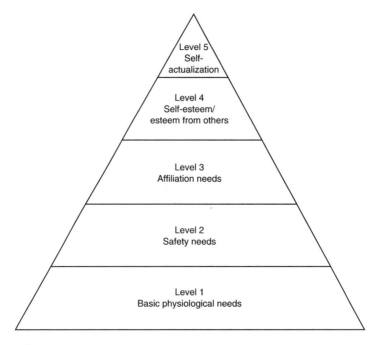

Figure 2

- Heat, light, food and drink, ventilation etc. (the basic necessities that exist in a home or an office)
- A reliable method of communicating with managers, colleagues and customers (where applicable)
- A security system (at the very least a lockable file cabinet) to keep office documentation and company confidential material safe and secure.

We heard of two diametrically different approaches to setting up remote workers. The first was sink or swim, where the remote worker had to find everything for themselves. When we expressed incredulity about this the remote worker concerned said 'You're surprised – that's nothing to how I felt!'

Laura B works for an established company supplying software training packages to schools. She works from home and travels around her sales territory training and setting up the software for her clients.

'It was hard when I started with XX. I knew I would be working from home, but didn't quite know what I'd need. The company provided a computer, email connection, mobile phone and printer but I had to supply a desk, chair and office furniture and organize a dedicated room at home. I felt they should have helped with this, and what is more, the first PC they gave me was completely unsuitable for the work I was supposed to do. I wasted a lot of time during the first few weeks getting this all set up, so I wasn't up and running as fast as I should have been. Later on the company completely changed its car policy without consulting any of the remote workers at all and this had a considerable effect on my personal budget. I resented this.'

There is a second approach which is much more sensible and success-ful. Here the employer is thoroughly involved right from the start. This is what Jan Carter of McCambridge Associates told us about how they set up their remote workers:

'We put the right infrastructure in place – both for business processes and technology. Although we wanted to work flexibly we still needed a solid infrastructure. We piloted this ourselves and this led to a

process manual which identified the technology and the processes we use. We supplied all the software, hardware, stationery and so on and we gave everyone training. We also have a probationary period where we coach them, review them and they can review us. This gives us discipline and keeps our standards up.'

The McCambridge approach was carefully planned from the start, Jan Carter and her associates had learned a great deal from their previous company FI (now Xansa), which was set up in the 1970s as an all-woman company using home-based workers writing software programs. Spotting the need for a way of working that would suit working mothers they decided that they would have a core team looking after the logistics and use self-employed consultants to deliver the product.

In another extract from the remote working manual of the IT company mentioned earlier in this chapter, this guidance from the HR department is given to people working from home:

You need to consider the following before making the decision to work at home:

Is your home suited to homeworking?
- Do you have a suitable room in your home to convert to an office where you can work effectively?
- Is your home free of any distractions that could affect your work. For example, if you have children, do you have appropriate child-care arrangements to ensure they cannot interfere with your work?

You will need to do the following before commencing homeworking:

- Contact your home contents insurance company to inform them that you will be converting a room to an office and working from home on a regular basis. There is no need to cover any office equipment belonging to the company (as this will be covered by our own insurance policy).
- Contact your mortgage company/landlord and tell them you will now work from home (in case of any additional charges – we will meet these if applicable).
- Contact your local council planning authority to let them know your home has altered status (in case of any additional charges – we will meet these if applicable).

- Ensure you have itemized billing on your telephone line, possibly consider a separate line and number to ensure that costs can be claimed easily.
- Ensure you have adequate power and lighting in your chosen designated work area to handle the equipment which will be installed.

As your employer we will:
- Provide a written contract of employment stating your home is your place of work and establishing your core hours of working.
- Inspect your home to ensure that it is suitable for homeworking and compliant with all health and safety legislation.
- Provide and install all the suitable equipment required in your preferred location and check that any equipment you use meets health and safety standards – see below.
- Insure this equipment against loss or damage (we will meet any additional costs incurred as a result of any increase in your home insurance premium because you are homeworking).
- Forward your post to your home address.

Your manager will ensure that you have regular contact with him/her and your colleagues as well as any information you require for your job.

Equipment:
Your manager will agree what equipment is appropriate depending on your job. You may be provided with the following equipment as appropriate at the company's cost:

- Desk and chair (if you wish to use your own it must be suitable and comply with health and safety requirements)
- Lockable filing cabinet
- Computer
- Printer
- Fax machine (if needed)
- Telephone and answerphone
- A second dedicated business line
- ISDN line or broadband access for permanent connection to our business network

- We will meet the costs of any minor modifications as well as making good any disturbance to home décor when equipment is installed and removed.

(This document is shown in full in Appendix A.)

Key Points

The most important point here is that the success or failure of a remote worker is determined right from the start of the contract. If the remote worker feels ignored or unimportant at this point then this attitude will infuse the whole relationship and they will never start to climb up the hierarchy of needs.

After the basic needs are fulfilled, the next concern is safety – not just physical safety, but continuity of employment, progression within the job, knowledge that there is a future in store. Here the remote worker is again at a disadvantage – out of sight all too often means out of mind and the remote worker does not have the day-to-day contact with the changes, opportunities, openings and developments within their organization that lead to progression. For this reason managers must make sure that all opportunities for development that are available for office-based workers are there for the remote workers too.

In our survey we also asked about the impact of being a teleworker on career development. The majority did not consider it had had any effect. However a sizeable 20% considered the effects had been mildly or strongly positive. The same proportion felt completely the opposite, that is, that it had been mildly or strongly negative. However, a smaller proportion felt the effects had been extremely negative (2.5%) than strongly positive (7.9%).

Laura B again:

'I really wanted to get out of teaching, so when I saw the job advertised it sounded perfect. It was only when I'd been with the company for a couple of years that I realized that I hadn't thought about how my career would progress. The job was advertised as working from home and there didn't seem to be any other option.

Because of this I don't know as many people in the company as my office-based colleagues do. In the two years I've been with the company my job hasn't developed very much. Over the last few months there have been several redundancies in the company and I can't help feeling that I'm in a position where it would be easier to let me go rather than someone who works at head office. This makes me uneasy and I do feel that my position has been badly affected. I was so intent on getting the job that I didn't pay as much attention to this factor as I should – I'd been in teaching for so long that I took the view that progression naturally happened.'

Pamela G, who manages a team of female teleworkers, told us:

'Most of them started teleworking while their children were young, and some of them weren't particularly looking for a career. We were aware that the company wanted to grow and that this group was a valuable resource to us. We put a development programme in place that used a mixture of mentoring, training and self development. Out of the original five workers we now have three who have moved on to line management positions and we expect that they will continue up the company.'

The next stage in the Hierarchy of Needs is really tricky for those managing remote workers – the need for affiliation, mixing with others, sharing ideas, solving problems together, identifying your place in your working group, developing friendships and feeling a part of the enterprise. Your peer group in the workplace very often provides valuable feedback on performance and fosters a sense of identity and belonging that managers sometimes fail to do. Making opportunities for remote workers to meet up with their colleagues should be a high priority on the manager's part. These meetings should be as evenly spread as possible.

Laura B again:

'We tend to have monthly meetings where I get to meet my colleagues as well as my manager. I like these, but they often have training and project meetings hooked on to them. I wish that the training and

project meetings could be spread out more so that instead of one great big session interspersed with three weeks of no contact we could meet at shorter intervals. I know that I can always call my colleagues, but I'm sometimes wary of interrupting them. I know that they often feel like that with me. When you work in an office you get to meet up round the coffee machines and as you pass their desks you can see when they can be interrupted and when they can't. It took me quite a while to get used to being all on my own. I use email a lot but it's not the same as meeting face-to-face.'

Here is a quote from Michael B, a remote worker who sells agricultural machinery:

'My boss expects, quite rightly, that I will get on with my job without having to call him up every few minutes. Obviously he gets to hear about the sales I make and the new customers I bring on board, but it often feels that the only time I contact him is when I have a problem. This came to a head when the outbreak of foot and mouth disease made it very difficult for me to do my job. Access to my customers was impossible because of the quarantine regulations, nobody was buying anything and no one had any idea how long this would go on. Although I knew that none of this was my fault, I got depressed and felt I was letting the company down. Fortunately my boss made a particular point of getting round to see me at least twice a week. While things were really slow he arranged for me to train the rest of the staff, spend time in the office, take training courses for myself and so on. We were none of us having a particularly good time, but at least we got through it together.'

After the need for affiliation comes the need for self-esteem and esteem from others. Feedback sessions again play an important role in this. The importance of feedback cannot be emphasized enough when remote workers are involved. It is surprising how much feedback actually takes place on a day-to-day basis with office-based staff. They meet round the coffee machine, take lunch together, can contact each other easily and can call ad hoc meetings to solve problems. They can easily get together after working hours to celebrate successes. With a remote worker it may well be that the main feedback they receive is during job assessment interviews, which although immensely valuable, are not likely to happen more than twice a year. One company we know which specializes in tele-selling cars has a running score of how sales are going on an electronic display board that all the tele-sellers can see, and when a sale is made they ring a ship's bell. Sadly this is not an option for remote workers.

So how can a manager make sure that successes and triumphs for a remote worker are suitably noted – not just by the manager, but also by their colleagues? Well, constant, specific and positive feedback is essential as is the need to mark successes clearly – written commendation so that the remote worker has physical evidence of approval is useful here and of course, always include the remote worker in all reward schemes and group celebrations.

The final step on the ladder is self-actualization, where the main reason for work is intrinsic to the person. Here the main motivational activity from the manager is to keep the remote worker interested and challenged. People at this stage on the ladder take pleasure in doing a good job, developing their own skill set, solving problems and working to their own (high) standards. Micro-managing people at this stage is counter-productive.

So, we can summarize the best ways to motivate remote workers at each stage of Maslow's Hierarchy of Needs as follows:

- **Stage 1: Basic physiological needs**
  - Make sure that all equipment needed is available and suitable.
  - Have a set of standards and practises that facilitate the setting up of the remote office.
  - Coach, mentor and review them during the set-up period so everything runs as smoothly as possible as soon as possible.
  - Make sure that all tasks and goals are thoroughly understood.
- **Stage 2: Safety needs**
  - Have a clear idea of how the remote worker's job will progress and discuss this with them.
  - Keep the remote worker informed of all changes, opportunities and activities happening at head office.
  - Review the development of the remote worker regularly.
- **Stage 3: Affiliation needs**
  - Include the remote worker as much as possible in all group-bonding activities both internal and external.

- Encourage contact between the remote worker and their colleagues.
- Visit the remote worker at home *regularly*.
- Try to arrange meetings so that they occur regularly, rather than in a great session followed by long periods of inactivity.

■ **Stage 4: Self-esteem, esteem from others**
- Publicize the remote worker's successes to the rest of the company.
- Include the remote worker in all reward schemes.
- Feedback, feedback, feedback!

■ **Stage 5: Self-actualization**
- Provide opportunities for self development.
- Set challenges.
- Allow them to organize their own way of working.
- Do not micro-manage.

And always remember, if the needs at any stage are neglected, the person concerned will transfer their needs to the one *below* the one that's missing, so if a remote worker at the self-actualization stage suddenly finds that they are being ignored, have no contact with their workmates, are missing out on group activities then they will fall back to the safety needs stage and will need reassurance and motivation at that stage before they can climb back through affiliation and esteem to self-actualization.

Expectancy Theory

This is based on work done by Victor Vroom. It proposes that motivation depends on the individual's expectations about their ability to perform tasks and receive the desired and valued rewards. The theory looks at both sides of motivation – not just the rewards expected for successful performance. This is particularly important in the case of remote workers where their belief in their ability to perform, plus the belief that they will receive the help and support needed for this performance, is a significant factor. Any perceived shortfalls on the part of the manager or employing company will have a significant impact on the motivation of the remote worker.

The theory is shown in Figure 3.

Here is an example of the theory in practice.

Maurice is taking his MBA at the Open University. He has a C+ average for the course and one more exam to do. He really wants to get a B

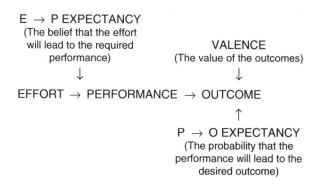

Figure 3

for the course and to do this he needs to get an A in the forthcoming exam. Maurice's motivation to study for this exam will be influenced by:

(a) the expectation that hard work will lead to an A in the exam, and
(b) that getting an A in the exam will result in a B grade for the whole course.

If Maurice believes that he cannot get an A in the exam or that receiving an A will not lead to an overall grade of B for the course, he will not be motivated to study particularly hard.

Effort → Performance expectancy involves whether putting effort into a task will lead to high performance. This will depend on the individual's abilities, previous experience, tools, resources and opportunity to perform. If Maurice believes he can truly work hard enough to get an A his E → P expectancy will be high and so will his motivation. If he doubts his ability his E → P expectancy will be low and so will his motivation to study.

Performance → Outcome expectancy is about whether successful performance will be rewarded with the desired outcome. In Maurice's case, if he is assured by his tutor that an A in the exam will result in a B for the overall course, his P → O expectancy will be high and so will his motivation, but if he does not trust his tutor, or has reason to believe that an A will not get him what he wants, then his P → O expectancy will be low and he will not be motivated to study.

The final piece in the Expectancy Theory pattern is the **Valence** or value that Maurice places on getting a B for the course. If he really does not care the valence will be low and so will the motivation, but since he really wants to get a B the valence is high and so is his motivation.

For high motivation all the factors E $\rightarrow$ P expectancy, P $\rightarrow$ O expectancy and valency of the outcome must be high.

Let's look at this in the light of a remote worker. Felicity is given the task of preparing a complex spreadsheet to calculate the overhead costs of selling and supporting farm machinery to her company's customer base. She knows that she has the skills to do it and that the time scales are reasonable. She also knows that any information she will need will be available to her. Her E $\rightarrow$ P expectancy is high. She also knows that finishing the spreadsheet is one of the tasks she is goaled to do, so her P $\rightarrow$ O expectancy is also high. However, she has not spoken to her manager for two weeks, does not expect her effort to be recognized and feels generally neglected so the valency or value of the outcome is low. Quite probably Felicity will put off starting the task as long as possible.

Acquired Need Theory

This theory was developed by David McClelland and proposes that as people develop, they acquire certain types of need. These are not inborn, but are learned through experience. These needs can be summarized thus:

- **Achievement**
  - Accomplish difficult tasks.
  - Work to very high standards.
  - Master complex tasks.
  - Perform better than others.
- **Affiliation**
  - Create close personal relationships.
  - Avoid conflicts.
  - Establish friendships.
  - Be useful within a group.
- **Power**
  - Control other people.
  - Have responsibility for others.
  - Influence policy and decisions.
  - Acquire high status.

People with high **Achievement** needs tend to be entrepreneurs, they like competition and excellence and will take sensible business risks. High achievers do particularly well if they are given tasks that are possible but challenging, where they feel that they control the tasks and get regular and fair feedback on how they are doing. They are quite happy working alone, particularly when they have control over the outcomes of their actions. They dislike tasks that are too easy or have no way of measuring success.

High achievers do well as remote workers, as long as they are tasked carefully – tell them what is to be achieved, not how to fulfil the task. Set careful standards that are very measurable. Feedback is crucial to high achievers – not just on their successes but on failures too.

People with a high need for **Affiliation** are more concerned with people and developing successful working relationships with others. They are 'integrators' and enjoy co-ordinating different departments and teams. For this reason, affiliation needs are often poorly served in the remote working situation – the primary need to be with others is thwarted and this leads to de-motivation. There are, however, situations where an affiliator would make an effective remote worker – where they act as a 'flying doctor' or co-ordinator of disparate groups, spending their time sorting out team's problems and acting as a go-between. Like achievers, affiliators need good feedback, particularly where they have had an impact on the teams they assist.

People with a high need for **Power** very often achieve high status in organizations and work towards moving up the organizational ladder in terms of controlling others. So long as the drive for power does not mean that the manager constantly interferes and directs the remote worker, but sees his remote staff as capable, self-motivated individuals in their own right there should be no problems. However, there is often a need in people motivated by power to be seen to be wielding their power and this can be counterproductive in terms of showing trust in their remote staff.

Planning and Organizing

Obviously planning skills are a key need for managers of any teams, however, when dealing with remote workers the need for planning and tasking has an added dimension. Because managers do not oversee remote workers in the same way that they can in the office situation, there is a greater need for careful and clear tasking, and indeed, a more careful examination of the tasks themselves and the need to examine risks and make contingency plans for any shortfalls.

The start of any planning process is to set objectives. These should be clear, measurable and achievable with a reasonable timetable. Once the objectives are in place, the tasks that must be carried out to meet them can then be defined.

For example, Pamela, an experienced trainer and designer of training courses, is a new remote worker with a multinational training company and has the following set of objectives:

> To design and deliver quality training courses on the use of database software to the personnel in the Data Processing Department of the company.

This is probably as far as the manager needs to go. Pamela's own experience will allow her to define how she will go about achieving her objective. What Pamela will need from her manager is help with the information and resources she will need.

On the other hand, Michael, another new remote worker with the same company, is not nearly as experienced. Although he is skilled at delivering courses, he has never designed them before and has never worked with a multinational company. Here the manager needs to plan in greater detail. Here are Michael's objectives and tasks:

> To design and deliver quality training courses on the use of Project Management software to Project Managers throughout the company. Three courses to be delivered per month, starting from Q2.

Areas of responsibility are:

- Researching Project Management training needs with the Project Managers themselves
- Designing the required training courses using the templates produced by the Training Department
- Delivering the courses within budget and to a standard of >80% success as defined by the course appraisal forms

- Following up the courses with debriefing sessions and corrective workshops where necessary
- Reporting progress to the Director of Training on a weekly basis.

Since Michael has no experience in researching and designing courses his manager will need to plan and if necessary organize the training, mentoring and information that will allow him to meet his objectives.

Key Points

The main point to remember here is to tailor management planning to the needs of the individual remote worker. One size does not fit all, and if the manager is to capitalize on the skills of the remote worker then careful thought about what is really needed, rather than putting in place cumbersome procedures that may or may not be useful is paramount. Since the remote worker is, in effect, in charge of their own procedures, the planning process should be a joint effort on the part of the worker and the manager.

There is an exception to this. There may be situations in which strict legal or safety procedures are an integral part of the task or project. Here procedures are not a matter of choice, they are a part of the job. In these cases the manager has the job of planning these procedures and implementing training for all staff concerned, whether remote or not, in how to use them.

Planning Checklist

Here is a planning checklist for managers of remote workers:

- What are the objectives that the remote worker must meet?
- What specifications exist?
- What are the parameters of the work?
- What are the tasks that must be completed to meet these objectives and which of these can be done remotely?
- What are the tasks that must be completed to meet these objectives and which of these must be done from the office?

- What time scales are involved and are there any differences with remote working?
- What resources do they need and are there any that are specific to remote working?
- Where should these resources be held?
- What quality standards must be met and how will these standards be checked?
- What costs will be incurred with remote working?
- What costs will be saved with remote working?
- What skills do the remote team have?
- What skills do the remote team lack and do they need training or mentoring?
- How will progress be reported by the remote workers?
- How will performance be reviewed?
- How can remote workers be involved with the planning process?

Summary

Remote managers need to have the same basic skills as those managing in a conventional office environment. This chapter has provided an understanding of these skills and how to develop them.

5

Skills for Managers: Feedback, Appraisal, Control and Development

The ability to give and take feedback is a critical skill for a remote manager. If the manager does not have first rate skills in this area then the chances of success for remote working are significantly reduced. Consequently this skill area has been allocated its own chapter separate from the more general management skills discussed in Chapter 4. Allied to feedback are appraisal and controlling skills, which are each given their own section here because these are areas that worry many managers new to remote working. The final section of this chapter looks at developing the remote worker.

Feedback

All effective managers have day-to-day or week-to-week contact with their team and through this will be very aware of what is going on, where the successes and failures are and what fire-fighting needs to be done.

They will also be running update sessions where they inform their team of corporate, market or local changes in working, policy or law and all the other changes that affect the workings of their teams. These are the day-to-day tasks of management and are quite separate from the annual or biannual appraisal.

But feedback is much more than just updating people with company goings on and swapping news. Feedback is the manager's best (but sadly often least used) tool. Feedback is extremely important to all business people, but absolutely vital to remote workers. Without exception, every remote worker we interviewed who had had trouble with working out of the office, put their difficulties down to poor feedback or indeed lack of any feedback at all.

So how do we define feedback?

The return to the input of a part of the output of a machine, system or process (as for producing changes in an electronic circuit that improve performance or in an automatic control device that provide self corrective action). The return to a point of origin of evaluative or corrective information about an action or a process. (Webster's New Collegiate Dictionary)

Feedback is the information loop that refines performance, corrects errors and rewards success. Without feedback, even successful workers lose their way.

Philip is the director of a successful research laboratory and is an extremely remote worker. His direct manager works in the parent company in Japan and Philip's laboratory is sited in England. He is highly qualified, very good at his job and the laboratory is successful. He told us:

'I never knew where I stood with my manager, I know that we were doing well – our results showed that, and when I wanted new equipment or staff or resources there was never any problem – in fact it was surprisingly easy to get any resources I needed. I sent him reports every week but I hardly ever heard from him. The management team would visit from time to time but there was no feedback other than an occasional pat on the back. I became demotivated because I felt my team was isolated from the rest of the company. I wanted to know how we could do better. In fact it got so difficult that I occasionally felt like creating a real crisis so they would be forced to give me feedback!'

Let's now look at the feedback rules.

Set an atmosphere where feedback is welcomed

Key Points

This is particularly important with remote workers. If they feel that the only feedback they are getting is negative they will not welcome or seek it and may become reluctant to admit to any difficulties they are having, which will only complicate the problem.

The remote worker should feel comfortable about asking for help when encountering difficulties and must know that there will be a joint effort to solve the problem.

Make feedback sessions a two-way process

When starting a feedback session try to get the person to whom you are feeding back talking within the first minute, this gets the two-way pattern of communication going right from the start. If the manager starts the session with a long statement which gives no chance for response then very often that is the pattern that will follow. It is a good idea to start with an open question.

Always have an objective that will lead to a positive conclusion

Your objective in giving feedback should be to reach a positive conclusion. The whole purpose of giving feedback is to motivate, encourage and enhance performance. It is not a ticking-off session or a venting of irritation. Here is an example of poor feedback.

Mary's time keeping has become poor lately. When she comes into head office for meetings she is often late and this wastes other people's time. She sometimes delivers work late, which holds up her colleagues who cannot do their job if her input has not been delivered. Her work however, is of a high standard and apart from these time issues she is a key member of the team. Her manager is concerned that Mary is seriously disorganized in the way she works in her home office. Mary seems unaware that she needs help with time management.

Mary's manager is personally very organized and has a short temper. When Mary is late for yet another team meeting the manager decides it is time for a feedback session. He starts the session by telling Mary how angry he is that she was not on time for the meeting, adding that her untrustworthiness and sloppy attitude is causing other people to dislike her. He tells her that she's letting the team down and unless she pulls her socks up he will seriously consider changing her remote worker status so that he can keep an eye on her.

Mary's response is defensive. She snaps back that if he insists on holding team meetings at 8.30 in the morning then he will just have to put up with her being late since she will not even consider leaving her school age child in the playground at eight o'clock on a cold morning. And as for the team disliking her that is not the impression she has. What is more, if he bothered to ask her why her last two reports were late he would find out that the database she is using keeps crashing and it is no wonder that this holds up her timescales.

The 'feedback session' comes to an abrupt end with both Mary and her manager no nearer to solving the problem and both of them feeling angry.

A more successful result would have been possible had Mary's manager thought about what he wanted to achieve from the feedback session, which was:

- to ensure that Mary came to meetings on time
- to find out why Mary's reports sometimes missed the deadlines
- to see if there were ways which he could help Mary with her time management skills
- to motivate Mary to keep better time.

Focus feedback on the sharing of ideas and information rather than giving advice or criticism

To state a truism, there are always two sides to every situation. What is one person's poor timekeeping may also be another person's desperate attempt to meet two conflicting and equally important deadlines. Mary's manager made no attempt to find out why she was missing time scales, and the feedback session consisted merely of him expressing his anger at the situation. No attempt was made to share the problem or even to solve it.

Focus feedback on the behaviours rather than personal traits

Making personal criticisms and judgements is counter productive and highly likely to lead to conflict, and aggressive feelings. So when you give feedback on activities that have been less than successful make sure that this is approached in a non-judgemental way and that criticism of personal traits is avoided. In the example given above the manager was very personal in the way he stated the problem. Words like 'sloppiness', 'untrustworthiness', 'dislike', 'letting the team down' are highly emotive and negative and are likely to call up an emotive and negative response.

Give feedback as soon as you can after the event

Praise or problem-solving sessions are best given when the events are fresh in each person's mind. Saving feedback until the event is a dim memory is pointless. If the feedback was to have been positive then the person needing it will have had time to feel that their good deeds have not been recognized. If the feedback was to have been about something that needed correcting, then the errors would have continued.

Focus feedback on what it may do to the person who receives it

A quick sanity check before giving feedback is to think about how you personally would feel if you were receiving it.

Structure of the Feedback Session

- Start on a positive note: 'This is what went well, and why' (exactly).
- Ask for input on what they thought went well and why they thought so.
- Ask what they think needs changing and how they would change it. Keep the discussion in the *present* time – no dragging about of bodies!
- Discuss how these changes can be organized and make a plan. Put time scales on the plan.
- End on a positive note.

If you need to give **negative** feedback:

- Give this in a non-challenging way. Keep your body language positive, no crossed arms or pointing fingers.
- Investigate why the under-performance could have happened, including basic factors like lack of resources, time, objectives, direction, or quality checking.
- Discuss how this could be changed and make a plan. Agree on your positive and possible actions.
- End on a positive point.

Job Appraisals

A Job Appraisal Interview allows the manager of a team and the team member to look back over the past months and evaluate their joint performance. It is an opportunity for the team member and their manager to approach the future months in an organized manner. Before an appraisal they both have the opportunity to think in depth about what they have been doing and where this will lead in the future; where the successes and shortfalls are, and what objectives they will set each other in the future. It is a formal and documented process and, if done carefully, gives a valuable *shared* yardstick for future actions and decisions. This is particularly important for the remote worker who needs all the definition of tasks, responsibilities and standards possible. It is also a chance for the remote worker to formally state any concerns that have not been addressed during the period between the last appraisal and the current one.

The appraisal interview serves several other purposes:

- to provide knowledge of individual performance
- to plan for future promotion and succession
- to assess training and development needs
- to provide information for salary planning and special awards
- to contribute to corporate career planning and progression
- to evaluate the efficiency of past targeting and goaling
- to establish priorities
- to identify, assess and resolve problems
- to assess and reassess resourcing needs
- to motivate or re-motivate the team member/manager.

Job appraisals need to be approached in a systematic manner if they are to be of any worth.

In terms of job control, the appraisal interview is one of the most useful tools you have at your disposal. It does, however, presuppose that you have accurate and realistic job descriptions for each of the people you will appraise – without these the interview will be very difficult to do.

Job Descriptions

Figure 4 gives an example of a fairly simple job description.

JOB TITLE: **DEPARTMENT:**

REPORTS TO: **JOB REFERENCE:**

Purpose of the job
Please summarize the main role and objective(s):

Scope of the job
Are there any quantities connected with the job (employees, budgets, tasks, volume, resources needed) which help to describe it?

Main accountabilities
What are the defined end results that have to be met in order to meet the requirements of the job?

Tasks and problems
What major tasks, projects and/or problems best illustrate the main challenges and achievements of the job?

Background knowledge
What knowledge and experience is it necessary to have to achieve the job's principal objectives?

Decisions within the jobholder's control
What decisions have to be made to achieve the principal objectives, and what has to be recommended?

Additional information
Please note anything that could give further understanding of the job.

Figure 4

Basic Elements Needed for an Appraisal

Before starting the interview you need to establish several things very clearly.

Goals and standards

These are the yardsticks by which the performance of the employee can be measured. Both the manager and the employee need to have a mutual understanding of what is expected of them; therefore the first stage in setting up an appraisal interview is to make certain that these goals and standards are written down and agreed. If there are no goals and standards in place then these must be decided upon and agreed before any appraisal can be made, therefore a job description is needed first and foremost.

A **goal** is a statement of results that are to be achieved. Goals describe:

- Conditions that will exist when the desired outcome has been accomplished.
- A time frame within which the outcome is to be completed.
- Resources the organization is willing to commit to achieve the desired result.

Goals should be challenging but achievable and should be established with the participation of those responsible for meeting them. For example:

> To increase the production of bicycle wheels to a minimum of 150 per day by 17 October. The cost of this increase should not be more than £100.

Standards refer to ongoing performance criteria that must be met time and time again. Standards are defined less exactly than goals and refer to such things as attendance, breakage, manufacturing tolerances, production rates and safety standards. They are most effective when established with the participation of those who must meet them. For example:

> All telephone calls should be answered after less than three rings, all messages must be recorded in full with date, time, caller and message written down in the telephone log.

In general goals apply more to managers and professional employees who engage in individualized projects. Standards are more common for workers engaged in routine, repetitive tasks.

When employees participate in setting goals and standards, there must be no mystery about how their performance will be judged. They should never be able to say: 'Why didn't you tell me that was what you wanted?' or 'Who thought up those ridiculous standards?' So check that both the manager and the employee know exactly what is expected of them.

Preparation for the Appraisal

Key Points

Preparation by an employee for the appraisal discussion is as important as preparation by the manager.

The appraisal discussion should be a structured and planned interpersonal meeting, not a casual conversation. A specific time, agreeable to both parties should be reserved and topics for discussion should be known in advance so the participants can prepare accordingly.

To help the employee to prepare, he/she could be asked to consider a set of questions like the one below before the appraisal.

1. What critical abilities does my job require?
2. To what extent do I fulfil them?
3. What do I like best about my job?
4. What do I like least about my job?
5. What were my specific accomplishments during this appraisal period?
6. Which goals or standards did I fall short of meeting?
7. Could my supervisor help me do a better job?
8. Is there anything my supervisor does that hinders my performance?
9. Is there anything the organization does that hinders my performance?
10. What changes would improve my performance?
11. Does my present job make the most of my capabilities?
12. How could I become more productive?
13. Do I need more experience or training in any aspect of my current job?

14. How can this be accomplished?
15. What have I done since my last appraisal to prepare myself for more responsibility?
16. What new goals and standards should be established for the next appraisal period?
17. Which old goals and standards need to be modified or deleted?
18. What do I expect to be doing five years from now?

Preparation by the Manager

When a performance appraisal goes badly, it is usually because the supervisor has not prepared properly or completely, or has not given the employee the opportunity to prepare.

Before conducting an appraisal interview it is necessary to identify and develop the items to be covered. Since the employee's performance in his/her current job is the central issue, you will need to gather all relevant information concerning job requirements and established goals and standards.

Next you will need to assess the employee's performance in respect of these goals and standards for the appraisal period.

Now you will need to:

1. Review the job requirements to be sure that you are fully aware of them.
2. Review the goals and standards previously discussed with the employee – plus any notes you have relating to their achievement.
3. Review the employee's history including:
   - Job skills
   - Training
   - Experience
   - Special or unique qualifications
   - Past jobs and past experience.
4. Evaluate job performance versus job expectations for the period being appraised and rate it from unacceptable to outstanding.
5. Note any variances in performance that need to be discussed. Provide specific examples.
6. Consider career opportunities for the appraisee and be prepared to discuss them.

Basic Skills Needed to Conduct Successful Appraisals

The ability to plan the interview and stick to that plan as far as possible

Unplanned appraisals do more harm than good. Decide what the objectives are for the meeting?

What are you going to cover and in what order? Draw up an agenda.

Make certain that there is clear evidence for what you are going to discuss.

Flexibility

You cannot entirely predict what will happen in an interview, you may well find that unexpected problems are uncovered. Be prepared to adapt.

The ability to listen

This is the hardest skill of all. Active listening means: listening *all* the way through each statement and never interrupting. Asking for clarification where needed and using careful body language and letting the employee *see* that you are listening.

The ability to ask open questions

These are the sort of questions that allow the employee to expand and develop their answers. They do not elicit a 'Yes' or 'No' answer. For instance 'Are you satisfied with your progress?' is a closed question whereas 'Tell me about the things you are particularly pleased with' is an open question.

The ability to create rapport and trust

This is a mixture of appropriate body language, careful introductions, careful paralanguage, careful use of space and appropriate feedback.

Clarity in communication

The *sender* of the message is responsible for the *meaning* of the message. Making assumptions, using unnecessarily complex language, using ambiguous or unclear language and being non-specific all contribute to misunderstandings.

Open mindedness

This covers the ability to understand and appreciate opposing views and attitudes, the ability to withhold judgement and the ability to differ without resentment.

Discretion

Confidentiality is imperative if your employees are to truthfully tell you what they think. Any information that will be passed on to others must be clearly signalled.

Tenacity

The ability to stick to the agenda, even though some of the subjects under discussion may be unpleasant (this is particularly true if there is a problem with performance).

Commitment to the employee's needs

If the appraisal is seen as a mere 'checking exercise' or even worse as a 'ticking off' session, the employee will gain nothing from it. The manager needs to make sure that the employee sees the appraisal as a chance to develop and expand, and that the manager is committed to helping this process.

This kind of commitment is shown by allowing the employee to contribute every bit as much as the manager, and itemizing (and carrying through!) the actions that the manager will undertake to reach the desired goals.

Pitfalls that a Manager should Avoid in Appraisal Interviews

Bias and prejudice

These are things that we often react to which have nothing to do with performance – such as:

- Race
- Religion

- Sex
- Age
- Education
- Family background.

Trait assessment

Paying too much attention to characteristics that have nothing to do with the job and are difficult to measure – such as:

- Flexibility
- Sincerity
- Friendliness.

Unbalanced evaluation

Overemphasis on favourable or unfavourable performance of just one or two tasks could lead to an unbalanced evaluation of the employee's overall contribution.

Holding the employee responsible for factors beyond his control

Look carefully at things like missed deadlines, going over budget, losing clients, failing to deliver goods on time; many of these happen because someone else in the supply chain or back-up team has failed, rather than the appraisee.

Other pitfalls to avoid are failing to allow the employee time to prepare, and relying on impressions rather than facts.

Developing an Action Plan

In an appraisal, there are five basic areas that need to be covered, these are:

- measuring results against the agreed goals and standards
- recording and recognizing the employee's contribution
- defining, and making plans to correct, any shortfall in performance
- defining and agreeing a training or development programme
- setting or resetting goals and standards for the next appraisal period.

You might bear the following set of guidelines in mind when planning the appraisal.

- **Don't cover too much in one discussion:** Prioritize, cover the points that need the most attention.
- **Collect specific, unbiased examples that can be used to support your points:** Be sure to leave room for discussion of these.
- **Develop some positive approaches to problem solving:** Negative criticism does not help. Appraisals are about the *future* not the past.
- **Provide praise and positive reinforcement for items that deserve it:** Be as specific in praise as you are in everything else.
- **Identify development areas:** Be prepared by investigating development tools that can help.
- **Prepare a list of new objectives, goals and standards:** These will be agreed on during the appraisal.
- **Plan specific ways in which the employee can be involved.**

Evaluating Success and Planning for the Future

Depending on the success or failure in reaching the required standards and goals, a plan for the next appraisal period will need to be put in place. This needs to be done systematically as each case may be different. For example, the employee may have achieved or surpassed the standards and goals and yet no position exists into which to promote him, or underperformance may be due to a physical or mental inability to perform, in which case contingency plans need to be made. Here is a model that you might find useful as a framework for discussion.

Performance	*Future possibilities*	*What to discuss*
Very good indeed	Promote to higher position	Consider and evaluate choices
	Growth in present position	Make development plans
	Broadened assignment	Review how responsibility can be expanded
	No change in duties	How can performance be kept up?

Reasonable	Growth in present position	Make development plans
	No change in duties	How can performance be maintained or improved?
	Performance can be corrected	Plan correction and gain commitment
Poor	Performance cannot be corrected	Review possible re-assignment or prepare for termination

Organizing the Interview

Attention to the following points will make the interview more successful.

- **Timing** for the appraisal should be set well in advance, giving both the manager and the employee time to prepare. Try to pick a time when there are no pressing (and therefore distracting) concerns that might take priority over the interview:
  - First thing in the morning – not the best: you may both be distracted by worries about what is waiting for you on your desk.
  - Midday – not the best: hunger may lead to distraction, there may be a tendency to cut the interview short as lunchtime nears.
  - End of the afternoon – not the best: there may be a tendency to cut the interview short as leaving time nears.
- **Do not plan more than two appraisals in one day.** You will be too tired to do more than this, and the later interviewees may be shortchanged.
- **Make sure the interviewee knows what to expect.** An agenda or covering note will set expectations clearly and also helps the interviewee with their own preparation.
- **Prepare the interview room.** The room should be quiet and you should make sure that there will be no interruptions (to either of you). Try to sit at right-angles to the interviewee – confrontational positions often lead to confrontational behaviour. Make sure there are enough assessment forms, notepads and pencils. Refreshments help to keep the atmosphere comfortable.

- **Clear the air of any previous aggravations before starting the interview.** This meeting is for appraisal and future planning – not for re-hashing old problems and irritations!
- **Have a flip chart handy for any ideas sessions.**
- **Prepare appraisal forms.** This is the written record of what was discussed at the interview. Both parties must agree that it fairly represents what happened and both parties keep a copy. This is particularly important for the remote worker as it acts as an *aide-memoire* and checklist for the coming year. When preparing the appraisal forms, make a note of all the areas and dimensions of the job you want to cover.

The Interview Itself

Create a relaxed atmosphere, and try to get the appraisee talking within the first few minutes. The appraisal is an interchange of information and ideas – if the manager spends too much time talking without involving the appraisee this sets a precedent and the conversation may well become too one-sided.

State the objectives for the exercise and go through the agenda. Use open-ended questions to get the discussion going:

- 'What was the most interesting task you performed in the last 6 months?'
- 'Where do you think you achieved the most in the last year?'
- 'How do you feel you handled …?'
- 'What areas of your work would you say need more attention?'
- 'What extra help do you need to improve in those areas?'

Probe if details are missed or the appraisee talks in generalities.

Ensure you review all key areas of the job. It is useful to use the appraisal form to make sure you cover all the points. Use the appraisal forms as triggers to discussion, not dissection documents. Try to put yourself in the appraisee's shoes; the appraisal may well feel tough to the appraiser, but just think how it feels to the appraisee.

Let your views be clearly known to the appraisee; now is not the time to be non-committal. Even though you may feel that some of the points you are making are negative, no one can correct behaviour if they do not know what they are doing wrong. If you have to point out a shortfall in performance, talk about actual behaviours rather than making personal judgements and work towards a solution rather than simply pointing out what went wrong. Point out areas for improvement and explain why the improvements are needed and how they can be achieved.

Encourage successful behaviours by using praise (being as specific as you can) for work well done.

Ensure two-way discussion by asking for feedback from the appraisee. It is just as important to review management performance as the appraisee's performance.

Summarize from time to time. Conversation is a linear process and it is easy to lose track of what has been said without stopping from time to time and re-stating what has been covered and decided.

When you have discussed all the performance issues it is time to discuss future training needs and development. Here both people should work together to set action plans.

If you have used a form similar to the one on page 59 you will have a 'map' of what decisions, investigations and plans have to be made. It is important that the interviewee is closely involved at this stage – *joint* decisions and plans will be acted on while 'manager imposed' or unilateral decisions or plans will not be readily accepted by the employee.

As manager, you should have researched possible options for the future before the interview:

Keep careful notes throughout the appraisal, you cannot possibly remember everything that has been said over a period of several hours. End the appraisal session on a positive note.

As soon as possible after the appraisal, fill in the appraisal form and show it to the appraisee, when both parties should sign the appraisal form. If you can do this on the same day you can then discuss any points where you are not in agreement. This is vital when dealing with remote workers. Here is an example of the experience of one of the people we interviewed.

Denise S, a remote worker for a design house, was given an appraisal interview 6 months after starting work with the company. She felt that the appraisal had gone well and that realistic and helpful plans had been made for the coming year.

'After the appraisal I went back home and didn't hear anything for a week, then the appraisal form was sent to me by email and it didn't bear any relation to what had actually happened. I was horrified. None of the things that I had been told I had done well were mentioned and there was a whole section about stuff we hadn't even discussed. Nothing was in the appraisal form about the things that I had asked my manager to change, and the plans we had made weren't in there either.'

'I felt that the whole appraisal had been a sham. I refused to sign it, but my manager couldn't see me to discuss it for another week because she said she was too busy. I had a week of worrying and I felt so demotivated that I started looking for another job. When I finally did get to talk to her she didn't seem to understand why I was so upset, she said that she had forgotten to talk about several things during the appraisal and that she had put her thoughts into the appraisal form afterwards. I did finally leave.'

Key Points

A bad appraisal is worse than no appraisal at all. Workers (and particularly remote workers who haven't got the option of dropping in to see the manager about things that worry them), rightly feel that the appraisal process is a serious and weighty business and that their future with the company is based on what is said in the appraisal form. The whole appraisal process must be seen to be fair and honest.

Summary

Of all management activities the giving and receiving of feedback is probably the most important. Without it demotivation sets in and quality slips. The job appraisal interview is the most formal of feedback activities and therefore needs careful planning. Remote workers typically receive less feedback than in-house workers, simply because of the lack of day-to-day contact. If they feel that a job appraisal has served no purpose or has misrepresented the way things really are then the quality of their work is bound to be affected.

Controlling

This is often seen as the most difficult part of managing remote workers. Many managers value people working at their desks near them where they may have a sneaking feeling that somehow remote workers are likely to be 'skiving', or 'slacking'.

In fact all the surveys we have read point out that remote workers are in general more productive and complete their tasks just as efficiently as office-based personnel. Indeed, several surveys pointed out that remote working often meant that longer hours were put in to complete projects and this resulted in an increase in quality.

Teleworking increases productivity and reduces absenteeism – but also increases working hours

- 78% of teleworkers considered themselves to be more productive. The main reasons were reduced disruption, reduced commuting time and stress and greater flexibility about when and where to work.
- 22% of teleworkers said that they had worked at home during their last typical working month when they felt too ill to travel to work.
- 69% of respondents stated that their working hours had increased, with 45% of respondents reporting an increase of more than 9 hours per week.

How can this paradox of higher quality of life but increased working hours be explained? One reason is reduced time spent in commuting, which can free time for both work and private life, and also greatly reduce stress. Another is the ability to multi-task – for example, hanging out washing during breaks – so that there is more quality time at the evening or weekends.

Project funded by the European Community under the 'Information Society Technology' Programme (1998–2002)

Since quality of work does not seem to be greatly affected by remote working, the issues of keeping control of individual workers is not an insurmountable problem. However, there are several areas where control is needed to ensure that remote workers can function efficiently.

The four stages in the control process are:

- Define the standards
- Measure performance
- Compare the performance with the standards
- Correct any shortfalls.

There are three types of control that can be implemented here that will help:

- Feed-forward controls
- Concurrent controls
- Feedback controls.

Feed-Forward Controls

There are actions that are put in place to stop mistakes or under performance occurring.

Rules and regulations

These are often created in an attempt to define work standards. While there is obviously a need to pre-define standards and some methodologies, the best way to do this is to keep them to a minimum. Self-motivated people have an understandable dislike of prescriptive rules and if these are too cumbersome they will undoubtedly be ignored or even derided. The best way to create a 'rule book' is to involve the people who will have to live by it. This is particularly important when dealing with remote workers. The manager cannot possibly know all the ins and outs of the home worker's environment. Yes, they can make sure that all the resources needed are there and that health and safety practices are in place, but a rule that might be easy to implement in an office might be impossibly silly in the home work place.

Risk analysis and contingency planning (see Chapter 11)

Before setting new tasks or projects, the manager and the remote worker should have an ideas session to think through what might go wrong.

The risks and impacts of these possible events are then weighed up in the light of how likely they are to happen and what the impact on the task might be. For the high risk, high probability events a contingency plan can then be made. These plans become very valuable when the remote worker comes across problems. Instead of having to react to the problem in a panicky way, possibly having to call an emergency meeting and find emergency resources, the remote worker has a solution already prepared.

Linda L, a remote worker with a video supply company, was targeted with finding seven customers per day for the next week and to interest these customers in a large (and expensive) exhibition that her company was holding the week after. Time was of the essence. Her area was to target the financial market.

She and her manager held a risk and contingency discussion and defined the major risks to the project as: (a) external events that would make the financial market uninterested in the exhibition, and (b) equipment failure. They drew up contingency plans. Risk (a) could be handled by switching the target market from the financial sector to education. Risk (b) could be handled by having a mobile phone available as well as her home office land line.

Lists of customers from the educational sector were drawn up and a mobile phone obtained. In the event the stock market went through a severe downswing and she had to switch to the alternative customer list in the educational sector. No time was lost and the exhibition was well attended.

Concurrent Controls

These controls monitor performance as it is actually happening, a sometimes difficult exercise when the worker is not at hand to be watched over.

Regular status reporting

This should be a two-way trade. Any difficulties, changes or worries should be immediately reported. The more crucial the project the more important this is. The manager should set up extra reporting sessions for business-critical activities and design a process that makes it easy and comfortable for the remote worker to flag up problems. A way to do this is not to focus on the problem (whether it is a shortfall in the remote worker's efforts or problems caused by the company, suppliers or customers) but to work towards solving the problem. Recriminations and criticism do not help, constructive planning does.

Quality checkpoints

When planning, tasking and doing the risk analysis, checkpoints should be built into the schedule where progress can be reviewed. This might be something as simple as a checklist, or as complicated as team meetings.

Feedback Controls

These controls examine the output of the worker.

Final inspection

Here the outcomes are checked against the objectives. If specifications have been involved (and it is not just manufacturing industries that have the need for specifications) the specification is checked against the result. This will lead either to a clean bill of health or a list of corrective actions that need to be taken.

Feedback sessions

These are particularly useful when looking at working practices. The remote worker feeds back to the manager not just the concerns they had with completing the task, but also what they have learned, both good and bad. And vice versa.

Customer satisfaction questionnaires

Customers, whether internal or external, always have the final say. Their judgement of the quality of work completed is the basis for future contracts. Check not just that the actual output was satisfactory, but also whether the relationship between the company and the customer is comfortable.

Summary

Controlling remote workers is not a problem when it is approached as a joint endeavour. Successful remote workers are motivated to perform well and will resent micro-management. The manager's job here is to control the dependencies that might hamper the remote worker:

- The supply chain to remote workers – ensuring that they have the resources that they need.
- Information flow – getting the right information to remote workers at the right time.

Key Points

Management control should not be seen as criticism and constant checking from the manager's side, but more as a two-way process where both the manager and the remote worker move forward to a successful conclusion.

Developing

Developing remote workers needs to be done systematically, working within the same development plan offered to every employee. As we have heard before, several of the remote workers we interviewed felt that they were often on the fringes of the development plans offered to people who worked on company premises, and that their jobs were sometimes seen as useful to the company but not expected to change much.

Examine the job that the remote worker was employed to do: does the job description match the job as it is now? There are very few jobs that stay the same from day to day. Before planning any development it is important to know just what the job as envisaged for the future will require. Corporate training needs must be taken into account at this point.

George is a remote worker for a company selling home improvement merchandise over the Web. He designs, produces and updates the Web pages that service this. Any training that he needs for new software is always available to him, and he likes that, but recently he discovered that all the workers at head office had had a two-day training course in how to run meetings (something that the company felt was sorely needed). He had not been invited. When he asked his manager why, he was told that he was part of the technical group and they did not think he would be interested. Quite why technically skilled people had less need of skills for running meetings was beyond George and he was left feeling that he had been pigeonholed.

Assess individual performance against current and future job requirements. Again, this should be a two-way assessment with input from the remote worker. Quite often remote workers may have skills that, although they appeared on their CV, are not necessarily used for their current job. It is easy to ignore these. George again provides us with an example:

'Before I joined my current company I had spent five years running a huge project for a Web design firm. I was qualified to use the most modern project management techniques and have kept myself current with these. In my appraisal interview my manager and I identified a position for a manager of a big project and I wanted to have a go at it. My manager seemed doubtful about this, but said that if I took training in PM skills he would consider it. It was only when I brandished my CV at him and told him about my track record that he began to take me seriously.

'I couldn't help feeling that there might have been other opportunities that had passed me by. Mind you, I was just as much to blame, I should have reminded him of my skill set more often. I had become so used to doing my job that I hadn't pushed myself forward enough.'

Once development needs have been identified it is time to plan a development or training programme. Here are some of the options:

- What promotion openings are currently available that would be suitable for this employee?
  - Within the group

- In another group
- Abroad
- What development material is available?
  - Training courses: Internal? External?
  - Secondment: Internal? External?
  - Self-training: Books? Tapes?
  - Manuals: Videos? Correspondence courses?
  - Sabbatical
- What projects are available to broaden responsibility?
- Is managerial responsibility an option?
- Is team leadership an option?
- What motivation tools are available?
  - Money
  - Relationships
  - Power
  - Job interest
  - Perks
  - Travel
  - Recognition
  - Awards
  - Status
  - Security
- What reassignments are available to suit the remote worker's skills?
- Who can help the employee to correct his mistakes?

When the plan has been made the manager then has the responsibility of not only seeing that the resources, time and budget are made available, but that progress is followed carefully and enthusiastically. Feedback should be sought on how the development plan is progressing, opportunities to use new skills should be found and praise where it is due should be freely given.

Summary

The remote worker's development plan is intrinsic to future success. Remote workers who stay in the same job for too long begin to lose existing skills and stagnate at a skill level that wastes their potential. It is also a key motivational tool. It not only fulfils the need for autonomy (a major need in many remote workers) but also leads to the spread of skills across the company.

A final word from George:

'Since my manager and I have been planning my development for myself and the company, things have taken a definite turn for the better. I'm now in a management position myself, running a team of remote Web designers concerned with three major projects. I still work remotely because this gives me an insight into the problems remote workers face. Our productivity as a team is high and our morale positive.'

6

Logistics

The fact that remote workers are based in locations remote from the main office sites means that the logistics of keeping them supplied with the day-to-day consumables, services and tools required to do their job are of a different order to a conventional organization. This short chapter looks at the logistics that need to be considered, *and put in place*, before remote working is implemented for more than a handful of employees. It is practical to deal with a few people on an ad hoc basis, but once the numbers pass double figures the costs associated with poor logistics will become excessive. Suggestions have been made to provide starting points for solving these logistics problems. However, anyone planning a remote working operation will need to invest in developing, possibly involving trials with small numbers of staff, an effective logistics solution tailored to their specific needs.

All these issues have a common solution, the logistical support needed to deal with a distributed organization. There are real costs associated with these activities and it is important to identify, monitor and manage them effectively. But, keep in mind that all the areas of logistics support involved in remote working have been solved before. Logistics is not an insurmountable barrier to successful remote working.

Key Points

With all these logistics areas it is a good idea to pilot the solutions on a smaller scale to test its practicality. It is much cheaper to evolve the right solution than it is to get it wrong on a large scale.

Two factors which have a significant impact on the size of the logistics problem are the scale of the operation and the pattern of work. These two are discussed below followed by sections covering post, meetings, transport, maintenance, finance and equipment.

Scale

The first factor that will determine the nature of the logistics implementation is the size of the remote workforce. The scale of implementations varies considerably. In this book the authors use the off-the-cuff definitions of scale given in Table 6.1 for determining the complexity of a remote working implementation. The comments provide an indication of the nature of the logistics problems that can be expected.

Pattern of Work

The second factor, mentioned briefly in Table 6.1, is the pattern of work of the remote workers. For example, a sales executive may work from home, but in reality is only using the home as a base from which to operate; the bulk of the time the executive is either in meetings at client sites or at one of the employing organization's offices. The logistics support workers of this kind require is almost zero. They would get their post from the main office or via fax/email and they would bring equipment in for repair. The facilities they need in their home office are restricted to sufficient space to use a notebook computer and a communications line.

Another person, for example a computer programmer, may be home-based 90% of the time and will only go to the office periodically. They may need logistics support, including postal delivery, maintenance, equipment delivery and collection, and health and safety and so on. Table 6.2 covers a number of roles and patterns of work and indicates the nature of the logistical support they might need.

An added complication to the factors mentioned in Table 6.2 comes from the fact that some people's work pattern will vary in time as well. For example, financial reporting periods such as monthly, quarterly and year end can produce bursts of activity, perhaps collating receipts that impose a periodic logistics load.

Table 6.1 How logistics implementation varies with scale

Size	Comments
Minimum: 0 to 4 remote workers	Implementing remote workers is logistically trivial, ad hoc solutions may be developed. However, what is done must work!
Small: 5 to 49	It becomes necessary to develop some processes and procedures that take into account the volume of material that needs to be moved around and the business needs of the remote workers and the organization. The logistics should still be fairly simple and will be very specific to the company. It is not expected that any significant investment in infrastructure will be required; geography is not usually a major factor
Medium: 50 to 99	It will almost certainly be important to invest time and effort in developing a complete logistics solution to support the remote workers. The nature of the home work, the extent to which IT is used and time spent visiting the 'traditional' office will have a significant impact on how much logistics is required. The numbers involved and potentially larger geography will make investment in a custom solution more likely
Large: 100 to 499	As size of the remote working operation increases then the importance of the logistics processes and procedures will increase too. It can be expected that infrastructural investment will be needed to deliver logistics support. Geographical factors will become more important as it is reasonable to expect the remote workers to cover a greater area. The additional costs associated with logistics to support remote working will depend on what already exists
Very large: over 500	Logistics will be a very major factor in determining the cost effectiveness of a remote working operation. It will be necessary to make considerable investment in both procedures and infrastructure. However, organizations of this scale will almost certainly have many, or all the components needed already, which may significantly reduce implementation costs

So, when estimating how complex the logistics problem will be it is necessary to consider the number of remote workers, their pattern of work and the effects of periodic peaks in logistics demand. For a large organization contemplating a change to remote working, this estimation

Table 6.2 Logistical support requirements according to pattern of work

Role/Pattern	Logistics requirement
Sales executive/ Representative	Small. These people are highly mobile, usually with own transport, their use of the home office is small and they are usually well placed to visit company premises as required. The logistics associated with supporting such people has been in place for a very long time and there should be no problem in finding best practice examples to copy
Service engineer	Medium. Again they are mobile, but will have a requirement for replenishing spares, returning items for repair, receiving items for delivery to client sites and so on. There will be a logistics support requirement for the equipment they use and possible site surveys for health and safety and so on
Knowledge worker (includes technical authors, computer programmers, journalists, accountants, administrators, planners, designers, and illustrators)	Small to medium. They will require more support than someone in a sales role. They may not have company funded transport and will require much more in the way of working space and equipment. They may also be based at their home location for a much greater percentage of the time, so they will need more support in terms of post, maintenance, health and safety and so on
Manager	Small to medium. This will depend upon the pattern of their work. They may be highly mobile as for the sales example, or they may be more like a knowledge worker. There will be a logistics support requirement for the equipment they use and possible site surveys for health and safety and so on
Trainer	Small to medium. Remote-based trainers will typically do course development and administration at their remote base, but deliver the training at client premises, training centres, hotels and so forth. In general their requirements will be similar to sales and knowledge workers, but they may require additional support relating to the delivery of training materials to site. However, this would be the case for office-based trainers and so is not really an additional requirement
Telesales and marketing	Small to medium. They mainly need a communications line and a computer. They may need access to mailing facilities if they have to send out follow

(continued)

Table 6.2 (continued)

Role/Pattern	Logistics requirement
	up material, but this can often be managed from a central site. There will be a logistics support requirement for the equipment they use and possible site surveys for health and safety and so on.
Home construction/ assembly	Medium to large. Although this type of remote working is not really the subject of this book, these are more often known as 'out-workers' and the subject of some controversy as they have often been exploited in the past. They are included here for completeness. Such remote workers require significant logistical support in terms of delivery and collection of materials and product, plus maintenance, communications, health and safety, site surveys, and equipment support. As discussed in Chapter 3, dealing with roles that are suitable for remote working, in most cases these are not, in part because of the high cost of doing it properly

process should not be underestimated. As has been stated before, the authors consider an incremental approach to implementing remote working to be preferable to a 'big bang' one. Allowing logistics strategies to be evolved and tested will give a much better chance of success and a much lower risk of interruptions to customer service.

Post

Although it is obvious once thought about, post and delivery can be a significant issue when remote workers are involved. It is easy to assume that all modern business takes place by email, phone and, to a lessening degree, fax. However, the reality is that a great many things still require the physical distribution of letters, documents and parcels. For example, legal documents still need to be signed, and there are over 82 million letters delivered in the UK everyday to more than 27 million addresses (source Royal Mail, 2003). A high proportion of these letters are business related and so remote workers are likely to need them. Similarly, despite having email systems most companies still operate internal postal services. Consequently one of the first logistical problems that needs to be solved is that of physical post. Two potential solutions are described here which can be adopted by a remote-working organization.

Surface Mail

This is the default solution. It requires no investment in a transport infra-structure to deliver to/collect from staff other than an in-house sorting service (which typically exists as part of most organizations' internal mail service).

For small-scale (less than 50 remote workers) operations this is the recommended approach for organizations that do not already have a distribution system in place. A combination of surface mail, commercial postal service providers and courier services will be able to cope with the volumes and time scales involved for most remote workers. That said, it should be a policy to adopt the use of email, or possibly fax communications in place of paper-based communication whenever possible as this is significantly cheaper to administer and deliver and has a much lower requirement in terms of logistics.

Key Points

In the case of internal communications, there is very little that needs to go by surface mail, other than receipts and contracts that require physical signature.

In-house Transport

Here the organization remains as the central postal address for all physical communications and utilizes its own transportation system to deliver and collect post to/from remote workers. For organizations where this already exists, this is likely to be a cost-effective option. Where security issues apply it is also a better choice than public mail services. However, if such a service has to be set up from scratch then there will be significant start up costs in terms of vehicles, staff, training and process development. It will often be cheaper to subcontract to a specialist organization.

[*Note:* See also the section on transport later in this chapter.]

Furniture/Equipment

Essentially this is a matter of delivery and collection to domestic property. There are no problems with this; every furniture and appliance distributor does this every day. However, there are costs associated with doing this. The economy of scale that goes with a single location is lost and this applies to both delivery and tracking inventory.

For implementations that are small (less than 50) or involve mainly knowledge workers, sales staff and similar categories of remote worker then there is probably no requirement for furniture. Where there is a requirement for office/work bench furniture then the options for collection and delivery include in-house transport, staff transport, or the use of conventional shippers.

However, almost everyone will have a requirement for computing, printing and communications equipment irrespective of which of the main remote worker categories they come into. The options are the same as for furniture, though for staff who only require a notebook computer and a mobile phone then self-delivery and collection is reasonable, except for housebound workers.

Maintenance

Again, because the equipment is distributed over a number of sites maintaining it requires more effort than it does on a single site. This should be kept in proportion; it is no different to the situation that suppliers of domestic equipment have in servicing and maintaining washing machines and the like. However, if the organization does not already have a logistics infrastructure to perform this kind of role then it will need to develop or acquire one. There are many logistics support organizations in existence that can take this role on, who will have everything in place already. Except for large scale implementation, it will usually be more cost effective to put this out to tender.

[*Note:* Putting logistics out to tender needs to be done very carefully. It is vital to have a really good definition of exactly what is required before starting. This is true for all procurement exercises, but in the case of logistics seemingly small changes in specification to the service user can have dramatic effects on the costs, and hence delivered price, of the supplier.

For example, a service to drop off/collect from the same fifty addresses within a 25 mile radius on a Tuesday and a Thursday every week will have a cost. This cost will be significantly different to one for a service to the same addresses but on an ad hoc basis any day of the week.]

The other issue that affects maintenance for remote workers is the ease of access to the maintenance service. The solution for this is to have an effective and efficient central point of contact (help desk) that can both respond to the needs of the remote workers and co-ordinate the maintenance activity. Remote workers don't have the option of going to find help in the building. If they are not to become frustrated and unproductive they actually need a help desk contact and supporting logistics repair system that delivers a working system in the shortest affordable time.

Billing/Finance

This is not an obvious problem at first sight as there is nothing a remote worker does that is intrinsically different here. Issues such as payroll notification, expenses claims and the like are essentially the same problem as that of post and are open to the same solutions. However, there can be additional problems associated with billing addresses where the remote worker purchases items that are paid for centrally but delivered to the home address. These problems can either be solved by an expenses claim or the use of a centralized purchasing department that can either forward goods received or arrange delivery. The use of centralized purchasing with a goods inwards inspection prior to distribution to the home worker can make dealing with faulty goods or disputed deliveries easier to deal with. Unless the added delay in distribution from the central site to the remote worker is an issue then there is much merit in this process for high value items.

There is not usually an issue in clients receiving invoices with a central address even when their contact is dealing with them from a home address.

Meetings

Whilst it may be practical for remote staff to have a meeting with one or two people at their home base, there are likely to be occasions when they need to be involved in larger meetings. In addition, it may not give the best impression to clients (not to mention possible planning issues) to have large or frequent meetings in a living room of a domestic property.

For these reasons remote workers need either to have access to meeting facilities at base offices, or to have an arrangement with hotels and such like that have appropriate facilities. In either case then there will need to be an effective booking system and centralized payment system if it is to be easy to use. Many of the large hotel groups can offer this kind of support. When choosing, geographical coverage, price, ease of booking and availability will be important decision factors.

Some years ago a petrol distributor that owned a large number of petrol stations set up office facilities in its retail outlets specifically for use by its own mobile staff and also for rental use by service organizations who wanted easily locatable, and conveniently located office space.

There can be further convenience issues where remote workers very distant from each other need to meet. In this case there needs to be access to some central facility at the central office, or similar location, for them to meet half way.

Overall, the meetings simply require planning in much the same way as they do in a conventional working environment, but the travel and meeting room booking aspects may be more complex. The solution is to develop efficient processes to support this.

Transport

This is part of the solution to many of the logistics points identified here. In cases where the remote workers have cars that are provided by the organization in order to do their job, for example sales staff, then these can be used to solve most problems without incurring additional cost.

Where an organization already has an established transport system, for example a retail distribution company, then it will be sensible to look first at using this infrastructure to provide delivery and collection facilities.

A good example of the options available for delivery and collection from remote sites was obtained from the equipment service division of a large European IT Company. All the service engineers were remote workers based at their homes, covering a territory in the vicinity of their home base. These engineers, there were about 80 of them, had regular requirements to return equipment to base for repair, receive spare parts and obtain and submit paperwork. To support this a delivery service was set up that followed a set route around certain office and the homes of key engineers every day from Monday to Friday in the afternoon/early evening. All the engineers had access to email and had mobile phone communications. So the standard operating method was for parts to be ordered from the centre and collected from the nearest key engineer or drop off point. This was also used as the standard return route. Similarly, paper communications could be distributed and returned this way (for example customer signed receipts). This service was delivered at a fixed price, irrespective of the number of items sent. In other words, if it was just used for one item it was very expensive, if it was used for a thousand, it was very economical. The service was backed up with courier delivery for urgent and out of hours items.

The problem was that it was easier for engineers to use the courier service than it was for them to use the delivery system, consequently the organization was wasting money on the under utilized delivery service. The solution to this was strongly enforced operating procedures to ensure that the 'exception' service was only used when it was really necessary. In addition, the benefits of the delivery service were publicized and engineers provided with an incentive to use the delivery service where it did not adversely impact the client.

Where there are a reasonable number of remote workers this approach can be of considerable benefit for equipment, furniture, spare parts and routine paperwork logistics. However, attention needs to be given to the geography of the delivery service drop off and collection points – in the example given all the engineers had transport and were close enough to each other to make local distribution practical. They also had both email and mobile communications for both back up and urgent use.

Policies and Procedures

All the logistics processes that are developed to support remote working need to be documented as they are developed, and reviewed on a regular basis to make sure they are effective. The elements of these policies and procedures that directly affect remote workers will need to be communicated clearly to all the relevant staff. Similarly, given the importance of having policies and procedures that work in supporting the implementation of remote working, it is essential that everyone involved has access to the latest copies of these. The same applies to notice boards. Logistics support will be needed to maintain and distribute this information. With modern technology this can be delivered via the company's intranet, or similar facilities, and should be a low cost item.

The scope of these policies and procedures will have to include anything and everything that needs to be delivered to or collected from the remote workers, and the escalation channels, error correction, exception reporting, performance monitoring and evaluation, inventory tracking and so forth needed to make the logistics work. This is a significant task in its own right.

Induction Pack

As mentioned elsewhere, an induction pack can be a great help when people are moving from office-based working to remote working. Part of the logistics associated with remote working will be the maintenance and distribution of this pack. Ideally people will be both given their own pack in hard copy and also provided with access to an electronic copy. It is essential that all the logistics processes-related help lines and so forth are properly documented within this pack. Not only should the information be comprehensive, but it must also be very easy to use – it should be clear to any remote worker whom they have to call and when they can expect the problem to be fixed. Proper escalation processes should be provided to deal with genuinely urgent situations as well as the run of the mill.

Costs

Although not a logistics issue as such, this support will be a significant cost driver for any remote working implementation. As part of the logistics process it is essential that the real added costs, or savings, of supporting remote workers are captured and monitored. As discussed in the section on transport, relatively small changes in usage of a logistics service can have significant impact on bottom line costs. These need to be carefully watched and controlled as part of the management of the remote-working programme.

Ideally, a cost model will be built up, perhaps using a spreadsheet, that is updated on a week by week, month by month basis to allow trends to be identified, and remedial action taken before serious cost overruns can occur. This cost model will form part of the evaluation model for determining the viability of a remote working scheme.

Summary

Question	Checked
Is the remote working population small enough to be dealt with on an ad hoc basis?	
Has the mixture of remote workers and pattern of use been established?	
Can you make use of any existing infrastructure to support remote workers, for example transport, intranet, Internet, email etc.?	
If procuring external logistics support do you have all the information they need to cost it?	
Are suitable meeting facilities available?	
Is a delivery/collection service required?	
Are logistics processes and procedures documented and up to date?	
Do they work?	
Have the logistics requirements of the remote workforce been modelled?	

(*continued*)

Question	Checked
Is there a need for the logistics processes to be pilot tested?	
Is there a defined support and escalation process for maintenance and other centrally provided logistics services?	
Can existing logistics processes be adapted to support remote workers?	
Is there a cost model for logistics?	
If collection/delivery required, has the best solution been identified?	
Are there special security requirements that will affect logistics implementation?	

7

Technology

As a minimum, most people who are remote workers will need the technology required to communicate effectively with their organization and the clients. This will typically be a combination of a PC and telecommunications: a mobile telephone, a communications line and a computer with a printer. There may also be a requirement for more specialist equipment relating to the job they do, for example maintenance equipment, credit card readers and so forth. All this will need to be implemented in such a way that the remote worker is able to operate at least as effectively as one who is office-based.

This chapter considers the support, maintenance, security and procedures that need to be considered when providing technology for remote use.

Information Technology

Computing

The most likely piece of equipment is the personal computer. This may be a fixed unit or a portable device. Whatever it is, it will need to be installed, set up and connected to the power supply, communications and so forth.

The specifications for such machines change very frequently – ex Microsoft co-founder Moore's law, which states that the performance doubles and the price of a personal computer halves every 18 months, still holds good. Consequently no specifications will be suggested here.

However, when defining the specification of a machine for use by a remote worker the following points should be taken into consideration.

Performance

The performance of a computer is largely determined by a combination of processor speed, disk space/access times, memory quantity/access times and graphics speed. Whatever machine is chosen now, a better one can be had for the same price in 3 months' time. However, for general business use, as opposed to specialist graphics and the like, a top of the range system will not be needed and the performance required is simply that needed to run the applications that the user needs. A minimum specification needs to be drawn up and then it is a simple matter of choosing a system that exceeds this.

Usability

Screen

The larger the screen size the easier the machine is to use. For partially sighted users, special screens are available to meet their needs. Allied to screen size is screen technology. Flat panel screens use less power and take up less space than traditional CRT-based devices and are to be preferred on both environmental and ergonomic grounds.

Back-up facilities

If data security and integrity are to be maintained, the remote worker needs a system that has built-in facilities for backing up and recovering data. This may be a tape or CD/DVD writing device or it may be via a central site accessed over a communications link.

Communication/network facilities

A remote worker will need to communicate with the main organization and possibly with customers and other contacts. Consequently the system will need appropriate devices, such as modem, fax and network connectivity to support this. Applications software will also be required to make these devices work.

Support

Where support for the systems will not be supplied by the sponsoring organization, then support from the equipment supplier is critical if the remote worker is to have an acceptable level of system availability. Support may also be an added cost item.

Price

All the features and facilities that are discussed here come at a price. Very simply the better the machine the more expensive it will be. However, it is worth noting that the relationship is not a linear one, particularly for performance. For example, when this book was written a 2.0 GHz (gigahertz) processor cost £80.49, a 2.4 cost £101.00, a 2.5 cost £147.00, but a 3.0 processor cost £497.00. There is always a significant premium to be paid for the top of the range – this applies just as much to screen size, disk space and other features as it does in the example given. Unless it is absolutely essential, always choose a system that is outside of this range as the cost premium is significant.

Portability

If the remote worker needs to operate on a mobile basis then a notebook computer is needed rather than a desktop machine. These systems often come with a docking station option that can be used at the main base to allow connection to networks, printers and the like without the need to keep reconnecting the devices individually. They are available with similar performance and options to a desktop system, but come with a price premium. Some systems have special facilities and features that relate to security and anti-theft devices.

A factor specific to notebook systems is their weight and size. As might be expected, there is a price increase for smaller, lighter machines. Sometimes weight reduction is achieved by locating components that are not required all the time, for example a DVD-ROM drive, in the docking station. Sometimes this is achieved by having them as separate, stand-alone components.

Key Points

For most organizations the IT department should be able to produce a specification for the equipment needed by a remote worker. They should also be able to specify the applications, operating system and so on that will be required.

Ownership

In most organizations the default decision will be that the employer/ main organization will own the equipment to be used by the remote worker. This is the simplest solution as it makes support, installation, maintenance, operation, security and so on as simple as possible. However, where freelance staff are involved, they may have their own equipment, also some organizations may consider this approach where the remote worker already owns appropriate equipment. Expenses relating to such equipment will then need to be taken into account, and procedures put in place relating to specification, support, application licensing, data security, data protection and so on.

Where the remote worker does own the equipment, then the following questions need to be answered prior to implementing remote working.

- Who will support/maintain the equipment?
- Who owns the information stored on the systems?
- Who is responsible for security/virus control etc.?
- How is access to organization systems/data to be controlled?
- Who will pay for upgrades/software applications?
- What expenses against this supply can the remote worker claim?

Communications

As a minimum, the remote worker will need access to a telephone line – even if it is a mobile one. More likely they will need something that is suitable for a computer to communicate over. However, there are factors relating to the nature of the communications needed by the remote worker that should be considered.

For the non-technical, bandwidth is a measure of how much information you can send along a communication channel in a given time. By analogy with a water pipe, the bigger the pipe, the bigger the volume of water you can get through it per second, i.e. it has a bigger bandwidth. So, on a low bandwidth connection it will take much longer to send complex information, such as a picture, than on a high bandwidth one. Predictably, high bandwidth lines will cost more than low bandwidth ones. The type and frequency of data will determine what is a suitable bandwidth for a particular remote worker. Cost is typically greater the larger the bandwidth. However, when assessing cost it is necessary to look at the whole package as there will be different connection, usage, quarterly rental and per call charges from different suppliers.

For example, a typical word processing document will be about 50 kilobytes (KB) in size. If this were to be uploaded on a typical 56 kilobits per second (Kbps) dial up it would take about 9 seconds. If the same file were uploaded on a broadband link at 250 kilobits per second it would take about a second and a half. This becomes more significant where pictures and audio are concerned. A 1 megabyte (MB) file would take at least 3 minutes on a dial up link, which is impractical for anything other than occasional use. A broadband connection would reduce this to about 40 seconds. Download times on broadband connections are even more attractive as the speeds can go as high as 2 megabits per second (Mbps) and a 1 megabyte file will download in about 5 seconds.

Remote Data Communications to the Organization

Typically this covers the information that the remote worker needs to access in order to do their job. This will include, but need not be limited to email, Internet, intranet, extranet and some organization-specific databases. In addition to text-based data, this information may have a greater or lesser graphics, video, and audio content. This mix needs to be established so that the bandwidth of the communication channel between the remote worker and the main office can be determined.

Based upon the technologies available in the UK at the time of writing, the following are the most likely options for connecting remote workers to base:

- Dial up
- ISDN
- ADSL (broadband)
- High performance dedicated lines
- WLAN (wireless local area network)
- Fax
- Mobile phone with data facilities

Dial up

This is nominally the cheapest way of connecting in terms of equipment and line costs. However, the drawbacks are that this delivers the lowest bandwidth (typically no more than 56 kbps).

Many ISP (Internet Service Provider) companies offer services that include all call charges for a fixed monthly fee – this will be cost effective for anyone who is more than an occasional user, which most remote workers will be. At the time of writing typical monthly fees were of the order of £15 for unlimited access.

The disadvantages are that whilst the line is in use by the computer then it is not available for use by the telephone. Either a separate line for voice use (land or mobile) is required or this limitation must be accepted. This can be a significant problem if the remote worker's job means that they need to be contacted by phone at short notice.

However, dial up access has a further advantage for remote workers who need to connect to the central organization from more than one location. This includes those who need to work on client sites or who are not always home/office-based. Mobile phone-based data connection is now taking over in this arena, including use of wireless LAN and related technologies.

Dial up access is only recommended for those who need nothing more than simple email and small file uploads and downloads, and basic Internet access. It is simple to set up and administer, and is inexpensive.

ISDN (and ISDN2)

For a long time ISDN was the next step up from a dial up line, providing two lines of 64 kbps (which can be used as one for voice and one simultaneous data connection or both for data as required). This has the marked advantage of providing constant access to the outside world via the Internet and allowing incoming and outgoing phone calls at the same time. The disadvantage is that the bandwidth is not so great as to permit much more than the same kind of activities that a dial up connection supports (though in practice it will be both more reliable and probably up to 20% faster versus the 'average' dial up line).

The main disadvantage is that the cost will be higher than any dial up service (ISDN2e was quoted to the authors at £142 per quarter plus an installation charge of £99 to upgrade an existing line in 2003). It should be noted that this is not a simple comparison, as some free calls were included in the quarterly fee. However, predictability and quality of service will be greater, and there may be savings in terms of not requiring a second phone line for business use. A further disadvantage is that it only provides access from the remote worker's home base – it is not suitable for remote workers who require mobile access.

Broadband

Increasingly available in the UK, but by no means everywhere, broadband (using ADSL or cable-based technologies) offers a superior service to both dial up and ISDN and has the advantage of allowing simultaneous use of the line for voice. A critical advantage is that the delivered bandwidth is anything from 6 to 20 times that of a dial up line. This means that large files are transferred quickly, on-line applications provide improved response times, and it is practical to consider video and audio applications.

For most remote working application the authors consider that this is likely to be the best option. However, as with ISDN the connection is restricted to the home base, so mobile workers will require an additional method of connection when not at their own base or organization sites.

[*Note:* In areas where broadband is not available it is often possible to have a high bandwidth download facility using domestic satellite technology. The costs are similar to conventional broadband but it only provides high performance connection to the remote worker. This is acceptable providing that the remote worker only requires the same level of access for outgoing communications as delivered by a dial up link.]

Dedicated lines

For those needing higher bandwidth or those in areas where broadband connection is not available, then a dedicated line (often known as a leased line) is a high performance option. This is an expensive option compared to any of the previous three and is likely only to be a reasonable option in special circumstances. Costs will vary considerably depending on location, time the line is committed to, bandwidth and so forth. A further disadvantage of these lines is their inflexibility. There are often long lead times for installation/relocation and significant costs if the remote worker moves house. It is unlikely that these will be appropriate for remote working implementations.

WLAN

At the time of writing wireless LANs (local area networks) were well established as an alternative to conventional LANs within a building or site. They were also in use across organizations so that, providing the remote worker was on organization premises they could connect into services using a notebook computer with a WLAN. However, their use at public sites, for example hotels, stations and airports, was just being introduced. In addition, standards to support both mobile phone data access and WLAN access were developing – this would considerably simplify the problems of both mobile and remote workers. When considering WLAN-type technologies for remote working the pattern of use as well as bandwidth and costs need to be taken into account.

Fax

Although not as universally essential as it once was, fax is still a significant means of sending and receiving printed information over telephone lines. It is reasonable to assume that most remote workers will need fax facilities. This can be either using a dedicated fax machine, very inexpensive for light use, either sharing the land line or with its own separate line if the fax always needs to be accessible.

Key Points

Fax facilities exist in practically every country in the world. Consequently the fax is useful for all those engaged in international activities. Organizations will often have a fax even if they do not have email.

Alternatively the fax facilities can be supplied entirely using software on a computer, using the computer's communication facilities for sending/receiving the faxes. This has the advantage of eliminating the requirement for additional equipment to provide the fax. However, although fine for sending, it is not always entirely convenient to use the computer for receiving – it is often easier to look at a hard copy and large numbers of faxes may take up a significant amount of disk space if not managed.

Mobile phones for data

At the time of writing the choice here is between basic mobile phone for voice only communication, voice with limited bandwidth digital communications (so called '2.5G' technology) and the newly emerged (but expensive) '3G' phones with higher bandwidth, video capability and so forth. The costs of these different services relate to the flexibility and bandwidth that they provide. The choice will be a business decision depending on the needs of the remote worker and the organization. For example, a 2.5G or 3G service is usually only justified if there is a requirement for the remote worker to have high bandwidth data access whilst on the move.

Because the prices for both 2.5G and 3G were very volatile at the time of writing no examples are provided here. However, they are significantly higher than for all the other options, with the exception of dedicated lines. Only 3G provides a bandwidth that is suitable for anything more than the equivalent of dial up access.

Key Points

Although all these mobile technologies were still in a state of flux when this book was being written, the essential points for choosing the right one at a given time are clear. Establish the pattern of current, and predicted future use, the bandwidth required and the budgets available (both capital and recurrent) then choose the best fit that is compatible with other technology within the organization.

In addition to voice and conventional data communications mobile phones also support SMS, better known as text messaging. This can be used for very basic written communication and is best seen as a replacement for the old fashioned pager. For business use 2.5 and 3G and WLAN technologies are fast overtaking this technology.

In summary, once the pattern of use has been established then it should be a relatively simple matter to identify which of the technology options discussed so far is most suitable for the individual remote worker. Once that has been done then the final decision is down to cost.

Communications within the remote site

For most remote workers this will be limited to the connections between a printer, a PC and the communications line. Essentially, just cables connecting it all together will be all that is needed. However, where more than one PC (for example a notebook and a main system) are in use then some additional connectivity may be required. This can be done either by simple cable connection, via simple local bus connections (for example USB) or via conventional local area networks.

For maximum convenience a WLAN should be considered. This permits PCs and printers to communicate without a physical connection between them. Radio waves in the microwave spectrum connect the devices with a suitably high bandwidth. The main benefit from this is in mobility and flexibility within the remote base. The remote worker can move from room to room, or even into the garden, and still have access to communications and printing facilities. This can be a boon where space is at a premium. For example, a room may be used for working during the day, but when children come home from school the remote worker can relocate to another room to ensure smooth family relations.

As mentioned before under remote communications, the WLAN can also be used when visiting organization sites to connect to services, offering a significant benefit over a simple physical connection. This is becoming more common and it is reasonable to expect this to be widely available by the time this book is published.

Key Points

Time spent considering the data communications strategy before implementing remote working will be time well spent, as the right choice can both reduce costs and provide a flexible, and operationally convenient service for the remote worker – a strong motivating factor.

Voice Communications

The other area of communications, though much simpler than data, is voice. For the remote worker this will either be via a conventional land line or via a mobile phone, though the technology does exist to support voice communications via the Internet. It is usually advantageous to have a line for exclusive business use. It is not practical for a remote worker to be cut off from communication because a teenager is hogging the line. Furthermore, use of a dedicated line/number means that it is practical for the remote worker to use a messaging service out of hours to preserve work–life balance.

Mobile phones for voice

The main factors to consider when choosing a mobile phone for a remote worker are the pattern of use and the facilities required. Armed with this information it is then possible to choose the best tariff and the most suitable phone equipment to meet these requirements. Large organizations will probably have a preferred supplier with whom they negotiate mobile phone provision and service.

Pager

Where urgent communication of alerts is required then the traditional solution was to use a pager (or message pager). This device either vibrates/makes a noise possibly supplemented with a short text message, to alert the user to the requirement to get in touch with someone. Its history is from the time before cheap, and nearly universally available, mobile phones existed. Pagers offered a cheap alternative, some with a limited text messaging facility. It is not usually required for remote workers who have mobile phones and its availability as a technology is reducing as time passes.

Video

At the time of writing this is largely included for completeness, as most remote working roles do not require such facilities and the technology to support them over the Web is not of broadcast quality. However, it can be done using a webcam, a microphone and appropriate software. This gives similar quality to the 3G mobile phones already discussed. If it is needed an appropriately qualified specialist should be consulted for advice on implementation.

Key Points

When deciding what communication technologies to adopt for the remote worker at their home base the end result will come down to a balance between cost and the convenience provided by the facilities supported by the technology.

Training

The remote worker must be provided with the technical training needed to use the equipment to support them in their job. This will be much the same as for an office-based worker, with the added factor of needing to be more self-sufficient when dealing with minor problems. The remote worker cannot wait for a site visit for a minor problem. For example, if a cable comes unplugged they must know how to reconnect it and how to restart the system so that it is working again. So training will need to cover not only the applications that they will use on their PC but also the basics of troubleshooting minor hardware problems.

This type of training will need to be developed specifically to meet the needs of the remote workers and should not be thought of as a minor point. Failure to provide the right training for the remote worker is one of the main criticisms that remote workers report as a negative aspect of becoming a remote worker. Also, a small investment in start up training will significantly reduce the time needed to get a remote worker up and running and will reduce the initial volume of support calls that would otherwise occur.

Technical support

For non-specialist IT workers, and even many of those, technical support for remote workers is a serious consideration. The logistics relating to a remotely installed base of equipment are much more complex than they are for staff all based in the same office. This sub section reviews the support issues relating to site survey, installation, maintenance, help desk and support service levels.

Site Survey

If the recommendations in the previous chapter have been followed then there is no need for an additional site survey visit as everything needed to support the technology envisaged will be in place. However, if this has not been done then there is a need to make sure that the environment, equipment is being delivered to is suitable. This may be a site visit, or it may be a questionnaire for the remote worker to complete – a lower cost option worth considering. Key points to be included in a site survey questionnaire are given below.

Power

Mains power of the required voltage/current rating must be available at the site and sufficient power outlet sockets are necessary. There may be a requirement to provide power conditioning (filtering out potentially damaging power surges and spikes). If there are known power problems (as, for example, in areas where local power is subject to occasional interruptions of a few seconds) an Un-interruptible Power Supply may need to be considered.

Telephone/fax

+ mailboxes

If there is no telephone line already installed (admittedly this is unlikely) then it will probably be necessary to have one installed. It may be preferable to have a dedicated business/Internet access line anyway that is directly billed to the business/organization that is implementing remote working. The practicality of this must be checked. Telephone sockets will be required in the location planned for remote working use.

Broadband availability

Broadband availability at the location should be checked. Even if the local telephone exchange has this facility there are distance limitations on the lines.

Location/physical space

The location of the working space within the building must be acceptable. For example, it will not be acceptable to have any equipment sited in a basement that may be prone to flooding.

The proposed location must be large enough and well ventilated/heated so that the equipment can function correctly. If not, conversion of the physical space may be possible. There should be sufficient space to allow access to front, rear, and sides of equipment for maintenance.

Legal

There may be restrictions on the use of the property for home-based working. This may be the case in rented, leasehold, housing association or other communal housing schemes and must be checked out. There may also be local planning restrictions from the local council.

Health and safety audit

A health and safety audit is needed to ensure that the premises are suitable for use by the remote worker if he/she is an employee as the employer may be liable. In particular this needs to include cable runs, ergonomics such as the location of computer screens, lighting and so on.

Access

Access to the site must be acceptable to permit maintenance/installation activities. For example, it must be practical to deliver equipment to the site without difficulty. Access must be sufficient to meet any disability requirements if needed.

Security

Are the premises sufficiently secure to meet with any insurance require-ments for the equipment/information to be kept there? Insurance cover may be dependent upon the physical security of the premises.

Installation/Changes

Installation of equipment on remote sites is more expensive than at a traditional office. There are additional shipping costs, even if it is only for the worker to pick up the equipment from a central site. Also, if an engineer visit is needed to put the equipment together and to provide basic 'get you started' training then this can be a significant expense.

As will be mentioned under Maintenance, it may be worth providing additional training to non-technical personnel so that they can under-take basic installation activities themselves, albeit with support from a central help desk, rather than needing a visit from an engineer.

The notebook computer, which can be set up and tested at the main site before deployment to the remote worker, can more than offset its greater equipment cost because of this. The equipment can be collected in a known configuration by the remote worker, saving an engineer call-out.

The authors know of at least one failed roll out of remote worker equipment where it had been assumed that just dropping off a pile of boxes and an instruction manual would be enough to enable remote staff to get up and running. This did not work and the organization's central support desk was swamped by calls for help. It also seriously demotivated the employees and damaged the quality of the work they should have been doing for the clients.

Maintenance

Remote personnel need more maintenance support than those who are based in an office. This is partly because they are remotely located and also because they cannot ask their peers for help for minor problems. Trivial faults and problems that can be solved without a call to a help desk will more often result in a support visit or a longer call. Part of the solution to this will be training the remote worker to have a higher level of technical competence to fix minor faults and be more proficient in the use of the tools they need to do their job independently.

Logistics is also an issue for remote maintenance. When a component or unit fails then it will need to be returned to a central base for repair/replacement. This will either require a visit to the central site, a visit by a courier service, an engineer visit or the use of a postal service. Which is appropriate will depend on the urgency of the problem. An effective central help desk will be critical to the support of the remote technology user.

Key Points

Remote workers often work flexible hours and may require support outside the normal office hours that are usually supported.

It is important to realize that if a remote worker's PC fails then they may not be able to work at all. Were they to be in a conventional office they might be able to use another PC whilst theirs is repaired. This is not an option for the remote worker and this must be taken into account. A simple strategy is to have a stock of pre-configured spare units that can be shipped, or collected, at short notice for their use.

Help/Service Desk

Essentially the requirements for a help or service desk for remote workers are much the same as for on-site staff. However, by the nature of remote working it is likely that service will be needed outside of normal 'core' business hours. In addition, help desk staff will need to be aware that a worker is 'remote' as the support process will be different to that of on-site staff. For example, if the problem is that the worker requires a spare part, it is not simply a matter of walking down the corridor. The processes and items such as spares holding and location need to be tailored to the remote locations.

Where an organization already has an established help/service desk then it is sensible to involve its staff in formulating support processes for remote workers at an early stage.

Service Levels

Employers need to look carefully at the level of service that is needed by remote workers. For example, how long can they still be effective if their personal computer breaks down? What is the longest acceptable time between a fault being reported and its rectification? The answers to such questions may be different for different members of staff.

In the case of conversion of office-based to remote-based staff it is assumed here that the appropriate service levels for support and maintenance of any technology needed to do the job have already been defined. However, these will need to be expanded to deal with the issues that result from not being office-based. This will result in modifications to existing levels, and also to the addition of new service levels. For example, it may be necessary to change the hours of cover, or to have additional service levels relating to telecommunications performance.

Once this has been identified, and agreed, then it is necessary to document it in some form of Service Level Agreement (SLA). This may be simply for internal use, or it may be for use with an external service provider. Either way it is something that needs to be monitored for compliance and maintained and reviewed to ensure that the specified service levels are suitable for the needs of the business.

Typical points to be covered will include:

- Hours of cover
- Time to answer call
- Time to fix problem
- Escalation procedure

It is important that the SLA, when met, will deliver a service to the remote worker that enables them to do their job efficiently.

Operating Procedures

For medium- to large-scale remote working implementations, where an ad hoc approach cannot be taken, then it will be necessary to develop appropriate procedures to support the use of technology by the remote workers. These will include both the procedures needed by the remote workers and those supporting them.

These procedures need to cover security, asset management, data management plus installation, maintenance, and support.

Security

When employees are based at company premises then security can largely be controlled by a combination of the site's physical and IT security staff. Even there it can be problematic as regular newspaper stories about hacking, virus attacks and denial of services clearly demonstrate. Away from the safeguards of the corporate base security becomes an even greater problem.

One of the more high profile examples of the perils of losing remote data concerns a senior RAF officer who left a notebook computer in a car whilst he visited a car showroom. When he returned to his car the notebook been stolen. It contained secret material relating to the conduct of the 1991 Gulf war (Desert Storm). Fortunately, this was eventually recovered. It was just a chance theft – but it would be interesting to know what were the future career prospects for the officer involved.

The following points should be considered when creating or reviewing a security policy for remote workers.

- Equipment – owned and supplied by the organization
- Data Protection Act compliance issues
- Password/PIN standards must be enforced
- Asset management
- Antivirus/firewall, data encryption
- Awareness of risks
- Central control of platforms/synchronized updates
- Data security

These issues are expanded in the sections below.

Equipment ownership

In order to keep control of the use of the equipment simple, and within the authority of the organization, it is convenient to have the equipment owned by the organization. Where this is the case then it is simple to specify rules as to the use of the equipment in the same way as is the case for an on-site employee. Such rules will include restriction on hours of personal use, what information may be accessed via the Internet, stored on the machine, use of emails and so forth. Owning the equipment means that no special procedures need to be put in place to regulate home use; they can be the same as for on-site staff.

Where ownership resides with the remote worker, for example where they are freelance, then careful attention needs to be given to the control of information on the remote system. This needs to cover intellectual property, security, data protection issues, back up and so forth. In particular there may need to be restrictions on use of the organization's email and intranet systems to ensure that they are not used for improper purposes.

Data Protection Act

Where remote workers have data stored on their remote bases that come within the terms of any current Data Protection Act then it will be necessary to ensure that necessary precautions are followed.

Information covered by the Act includes such things as personal data (names, addresses, contact details), financial information, medical records and the like. A mailing list would certainly come within this category, as would a human resources department personnel file.

[*Note:* When sending out an email shot the sender should ensure that the recipient only sees his or her own address and contact information, not the rest of the people on the list. Use of an email 'blind copy' facility is useful here.]

Password/PIN standards

All the processes needed for password and PIN protection (or whatever other access security controls used) apply for remote workers. These should include regular changing of passwords, not using names or other easily guessable passwords and so on. Passwords should never be written down and staff should not disclose them to third parties. Central checks should be made to ensure that good practice is kept up to maintain security.

Asset management

Most organizations will have their own standards for asset management, and these will often include procedures for notebook computers and other mobile equipment. Where this is the case they will usually be suitable for dealing with the asset management requirements for remote workers. A short review to check this is the case will suffice. Where no such procedures exist they will need to be developed.

Key Points

Level of tracking versus practicality. It may not be worth tracking low value items. Also, for maintenance the ability to swap items for repair may be more important than knowing where every component is.

Antivirus/Internet security/firewalls/data encryption

If an organization already has adequate IT security tools in place then these should automatically be used for remote working staff members. However, they may not always be appropriate, or sufficient for use via public access communications and an IT security audit should be carried out to make sure that appropriate security measures are put in place. In the case of sensitive information, some form of data encryption may be appropriate. This may be particularly relevant where notebook computers are used, as they are often targeted for theft.

Remote workers need to be trained in the use of the various products, in particular if they require to be updated manually, for example from a supplier's website, then it is important that they know how to do this. New viruses are always being created and it is essential that the products designed to protect against them are kept up to date.

Ideally as much of this as possible needs to be either automated or controlled from the central site when the remote worker connects for email/data access.

Staff awareness

If any security system is going to be effective then it is vital that the staff involved are aware of the importance of security and the part they have to play. It is of little value having a comprehensive set of firewall and antivirus products together with sophisticated back-up systems if they are not used correctly. Even when staff use all the security tools, they can completely undermine security with a single careless email to an outside party. Regular staff briefings and refresher training/publicity are needed. There are many examples of effective security procedures that are taught as a one-off when someone joins the organization but are never followed up afterwards. The results are predictable, and potentially very expensive in terms of both cost and reputation.

Central control

A major issue with distributed, remote, workforces is that of keeping them all working on a common platform. Essentially this is a support problem. A customer service desk will find it very hard to deal effectively with fault calls if they do not know the basic configuration of the equipment/software that the remote workers have. As for office-based staff this is a configuration and control exercise; all systems within the organization need to be on a common IT platform that ensures systems are compatible with each other.

On-site workers are easier to control, but remote workers are far more at risk from the temptation to load their own applications. For example, it is tempting to allow use of a home-based machine for family use. This can result in the introduction of uncontrolled software that may give opportunities for the introduction of viruses or the theft of confidential data. It is preferable to offer the use of a second machine on advantageous rates rather than risk security breaches.

Data security

In this case it is the security and integrity of the data that is the issue. This means having a practical and effective method for backing up the data and for retrieving it in case of equipment failure, damage, theft or terrorism. For example this back up might be to a local CD/DVD disk writer or to a central site via a communications link. The actual method chosen will depend on the quantity of data and the frequency with which it is changed. If possible the process should be automated with the user being prompted to run the back up and a log being kept to show that it has been done. If the organization does not have suitable expertise in house to advise on data security, then such expertise should be brought in.

A regular part of any data back-up process should be a test that the data can be recovered. Periodically the user should be instructed to test that backed-up data is recoverable. This should be automated as far as possible or the remote worker needs to be given sufficient training to ensure they can carry out the test.

Key Points

In all cases a view needs to be taken of the cost of losing the information versus the cost of ensuring that it is kept secure.

Access control

Passwords, PIN codes and biometric devices can all be used to restrict access to equipment used by the remote worker that needs to be kept secure.

Data encryption and protection of data

When storing information on a personal computer, or sending it over a public data network, it should be kept in mind that this data may be accessible to others who do not have a right to view it. Where such information is needed by the remote worker then data encryption technology should be considered.

In addition, the physical protection of media (such as floppy disk, CD, DVD, tape and printed material) needs to be considered. This may mean the provision of secure, and fire resistant storage on the remote site.

Data management

The processes associated with managing information on the remote site need to be secure too. If not, then the data itself will be at risk. Data management processes need to make sure that the data accessible to the remote worker is up to date and that any changes the remote worker makes to the data are reflected throughout the organization in a sufficiently timely manner to meet operational needs.

Disposal of equipment

When equipment becomes obsolete it is important that no sensitive information, or information covered by the Data Protection Act, is left on it for others to access. This also applies to application software. Failure to remove the software may well be a breach of licensing agreements if it allows it to be used by those who have not paid for the privilege. It is not sufficient to simply use the operating system to delete the data. If guaranteed deletion is required then specialist software/techniques may be needed. As a minimum all hard disks should be reformatted to minimize risk of data recovery by a third party in the future. This is a task that should be specified by the organization's IT specialists. If there is none within the organization then a specialist supplier should be contacted.

Business continuity

The policy here has to look at what is needed to keep the operation running in the event of various levels of failure. Essentially this is a balancing act between the cost of providing cover for an event, the likelihood of its occurring and the impact of the event on the organization (see also Chapter 11 on risk).

There are two main elements to business continuity as far as remote working is concerned. The first concerns backing up the information and the second concerns provision of the facilities needed by the remote worker to do the job in case of major events, for example a fire at the remote premises destroying all the equipment/information on the site.

Fortunately it can be both simple and inexpensive to provide both of these for the majority of workers using readily available information technology. For example, if all remote information is backed up on a daily basis to a central site (and if email is also stored in this central facility) then it is relatively simple for the remote worker to access this information if the remote site becomes unavailable. This is true even if the remote worker's IT equipment is destroyed or stolen, providing suitable spares are available at the main site. The remote worker simply relocates to the central site.

However, it is also important to consider what needs to be done if the central site becomes unavailable to the remote worker. What level of locally stored information is needed to allow the remote worker to operate for a short period of time without the central site?

Audits

However good a security implementation is, or to whatever level it is needed, it is important to revisit the policy on a regular basis. The security needs of the organization, its customers and staff change with time. Similarly the threats posed by outside agencies, their abilities and targets also change. Consequently, what was appropriate at the time the policy was implemented may not be the case some time later. The answer to this is to have periodic audits of the policy covering the same ground as when defining the policy in the first place. Such an audit will include policies and procedures, reviews of reported failures in security and so forth. The frequency of such audits will depend upon the overall level of security identified when determining the initial requirements. By default it is suggested that this should be done at least once a year.

Testing

As with the need to audit the security requirements, policies and procedures described above it is also necessary to make periodic checks upon the effectiveness of the security. All that is required is to periodically check that the procedures work and are being followed. These should be recorded and it is good practice to simulate a real emergency from time to time to test the ongoing validity of the procedures. For example, a remote worker's access to the central site could be disabled for a period of time to see if the procedures are followed and that they work as expected.

Asset Management

This is another significant problem for remote worker's equipment. Asset management is the process of keeping track of all the equipment that a company has, irrespective of whether it is in the field or at an office site. This is never easy and many large organizations would find it difficult to say that they knew where every PC was at a given time.

Indeed, one of the authors worked on an outsourcing programme for asset management at a major retail financial organization where they had to institute a site by site audit before they could say what equipment they actually owned. Prior to that audit they only reckoned on an accuracy of about 85%. This was without any significant amount of portable equipment such as notebook PCs.

As a minimum all 'major' items, such as notebook computers and mobile phones, should be tagged and tracked to the level of who has them and where they are based. This implies a central facility, probably associated with a help desk, which has appropriate systems to track equipment moves and spares for maintenance activities.

The definition of 'major' should be defined by something simple, such as cost; it can easily end up costing more than the equipment is worth in tracking items such as mice and keyboards.

Data Management

Data management is always an issue in any organization. Information is critical for most businesses and it is usually unacceptable to allow its loss. Consequently it is necessary to make sure that remote workers have access to a practical method for keeping their data safe and up to date.

Summary

The benefits of remote and mobile working relate to the freedom in time and location that comes from being outside the conventional office environment. The operating procedures that are developed to ensure reasonable levels of security and control must always keep this in mind. For example, making a remote worker report in every time they took their notebook to a new location would make the life of a remote worker so circumscribed that they might as well be office-based – all of the costs with none of the benefits.

Other Equipment

Under this heading comes photocopiers, fax machines, air conditioning, and specialist equipment required to do the job. As with the IT equipment, what is required is a set of operational procedures that will ensure the equipment delivers what is required to support the remote worker in doing their job effectively. In addition, particularly where chemicals and other 'substances hazardous to health' are involved (for example in a photocopier) then the procedures will need to meet current health and safety at work regulations.

Summary

The starting point for deciding what technology is required for a remote worker is to assume that they require exactly the same things as a site-based worker. Then identify the extra items they need to maintain communication with the outside world. Next determine what they need to ensure that the information they have is secure in terms of storage and access and that any business continuity requirements can be met. Finally make sure that not only does it work but that the remote worker is happy to work with it. Technology is an enabler of remote working, but it does need to be effectively managed.

Question	Checked
Has a technical specification been defined for remote workers?	
Has all the equipment needed by the remote worker been identified?	
Has it been specified sufficiently well so it can be procured?	
What is capital and recurrent cost associated with this equipment?	
Has the technical training requirement been defined?	
Is technical training available for remote staff?	
Is the support process defined and in place?	
Are communications requirements/costs defined?	
Has this been turned into a communications strategy for remote workers?	
Are site survey requirements defined?	

(*continued*)

Question	Checked
Is the site survey completed?	
Did the remote site meet requirements?	
If not, is it cost-effective to remedy this?	
Are security requirements defined?	
Are asset management requirements and process in place?	
Are back-up/data restoration processes in place for remote working?	
Have appropriate technical security software and processes been put in place?	
Is refresher training on security scheduled?	

8

Personal Skills for the Remote Worker

It stands to reason that anyone working from home must have all the skills that they would need if they were doing the same job from an office. However there are certain skills that become particularly important to the remote worker:

- Time management
- Self-organization
- Self-motivation
- Communication skills
- Problem solving and decision making

This chapter looks at these skills in the light of remote working. We make no apology for including a long section on time management since this was the prime skill identified by the remote workers we interviewed.

Janet, a remote worker with a company specializing in research for the oil industry told us: 'After many years working in a well run office, I became a remote worker two years ago. Bearing in mind that most of the work I do is desk- and Web-based I thought it would be easy to transfer my job to my home workplace without much alteration. I was really surprised to find how many support tasks I had taken for granted in the office. There was no switchboard to filter incoming telephone calls, no coffee constantly on tap, stationery supplies needed ordering and organizing, the post room wasn't there, even relatively simple tasks like filing and tidying became much harder when I was working in a smaller space. I thought that my time management was good – but I realized that I would have to be much more organized in my home office.'

Time Management

The essence of good time management is:

- Clearly knowing what has to be done
- Knowing how long things will take
- Prioritizing tasks
- Identifying time waster
- Stopping procrastination

It is not rocket science and you do not need costly or complicated tools, although that said, Microsoft's Outlook™ is a very useful package indeed, having the tools that can do most of the things that good time management demands.

Clearly Knowing What has to be Done

Task definition is extremely important to the remote worker – at the office any lack of clarity is easily resolved by discussion with others or popping round to talk to the manager about what is unclear. Since this is not an option for the remote worker it is all too easy to start ill-defined tasks without knowing what the expected result is to be. Here is an example:

John X, a remote worker for a software company, had been asked to prepare a report for a customer on the expected levels of service in a maintenance contract. He had done this several times before and expected it to be a fairly routine task. He couldn't contact the salesperson concerned but started anyway, taking a day to draft out the report. It was only then that he discovered that this was a one-off contract, which was completely untypical. He'd wasted a day because he couldn't contact the person who had the vital information, and the briefing that he had been given was inadequate to say the least.

What he should have done was to interrogate the manager who set him the task.

- What was the work to be done – exactly?
- What was the result to be?
- Were there any unusual circumstances that affected the work?
- What time scales were involved?
- Whom could he contact if he needed any other information?

Key Points

It is essential to get into the habit of clarifying tasks *at the time when they are passed to the remote worker.*

Once the tasks have been clearly defined they need to be listed in a Day Book or task list. (A Day Book is a bound book in which the remote worker keeps all tasks, actions, notes and so on as a permanent record.)

These are the things to list:

- business tasks
- 'housekeeping' tasks
- promised actions (from the worker)
- promised actions (to the worker)
- fixed tasks/meetings
- fixed times (eating/travelling)
- deadlines
- anniversaries/congratulations
- delegated tasks
- tasks that need checking
- contact numbers/addresses
- file names/locations
- research/thinking time
- holidays
- personal appointments
- exceptions

Knowing How Long Tasks Will Take

Tasks can be divided into three kinds: infrastructure, domestic and revenue earning.

- **Infrastructural** tasks are things like: returning telephone calls, discussions, internal mail, external mail, meetings, answering the phone, training, reporting, travelling and so on.
- **Domestic** tasks are things like: filing, tidying, finding information, doing expenses, coffee and tea breaks, parking, ordering supplies, chit chat and so forth.
- **Revenue earning** tasks are things like: selling, providing services to customers, demonstrating, managing projects, meeting clients, marketing, presenting to clients, invoicing, and so on.

The first thing that needs to be said is that the infrastructural and domestic tasks support the revenue earning tasks and so must not be neglected. Secondly, remote workers very often have to do a great deal more of the infrastructural and domestic tasks than office-based workers. Thirdly, it is a common failing to underestimate the amount of time needed for these tasks. As a rule of thumb, at least the equivalent of one and a half working days a week will be spent on them. The best way to learn how long tasks actually take is to keep a diary (with times marked in) of everything that is done at work for three or four days and examine it carefully. This can then act as a guide for working out how much time to allocate for tasks when planning the working day or estimating time scales for projects.

Prioritizing Tasks

Having worked out what tasks need to be done, it is now necessary to prioritize them. It is important to look at each task and ask these questions:

- **Importance**
  - Do other activities depend on this task?
  - Do other people depend on this task being completed?
  - Does the value of this task outweigh the value of other tasks?

Key Points

Whether you like or hate this task has nothing to do with its importance!

- **Imminence**
  - Must this task be done by a particular time?
  - Is there a deadline for this task?

Key Points

Whether you want to do this task or have been putting it off has nothing to do with its imminence!

- **Fixed or movable**
  - Is this task fixed to a set timetable? (end of month reports, weekly group meetings ...)
  - Can it be moved (having a drink with friends after work)?
  - What is the return on effort?
  - How much will doing this task repay the company in terms of profit, time saved, smooth running of business (for example, would backing up the information on a PC bring more benefits than reading a back copy of *Business Weekly*?)

When the tasks have been examined they can then be prioritized:

1. first, in order of imminence
2. then in order of importance
3. then fixed items
4. then movable items
5. then items with a high return
6. then items with a low return.

Particular attention needs to be paid to dependencies.

- Which tasks need other task's input or tasks from another person?
- Which tasks are people waiting for before they can get on with their tasks?
- What deadlines exist?

With all this information the task list can be prioritized and the following options considered:

- Do it now.
- Delegate it (this is often a harder option for a remote worker than it would be for someone based in the office).
- Put it off until later.
- Don't do it at all.

Identifying Time Wasters and Fixing the Problem

This section covers practical advice for the home worker on how to organize information and how to keep things in control.

Organizing information

One of the greatest time wasters in business is losing things. The solution is efficient filing (no stacking) at least once a day if possible, constant tidying and better file control.

Different types of information should be organized in appropriate ways, as follows:

Alphabetical	General filing
Topic or subject	Projects
Geographical	Territories/sales
Chronological	Phone call/account records
Numerical	Invoicing/purchasing etc
Tickler file	12 folders (1 per month)
	31 folders (1 per day)

Here are some suggestions as to how to keep information well organized:

- At the start of each month, place items in daily slots, place month file at front, then day files behind, then other month files behind these.
- Create a dump drawer and use it for low payoff, non-time-critical paperwork. Clear it out once a month.
- Create a 'Short Term Parking Space', a designated place where visitors or family are allowed to put things on your desk, and don't allow them to put things anywhere else.

- Make a 'filing map' and an index – keep this in view.
- Do the same with your computer disks, and the information held on your hard disk.
- Print out the file names of each and every disk and folder at least once a month and note what is in them.
- Print a header or footer on every page you generate on the computer containing this info: disk name or number, program name, folder name, file name, page number For example: (C:\word\TIME TOWIN\ TIMECARD\12\SS). If necessary add the originator's initials.
- Use sensible and understandable file names.
- Back up your disks regularly and label them clearly with the contents and date. (Do not store the back-up disks with your computer!)
- Put all maps and reminder lists in your day book and only have the stuff you are working with on the desk.

The telephone

Again, this is a great time waster if calls are handled carelessly and, of course, it is a temptation to remote workers who miss the day-to-day conversations that occur in the office.

Try to follow these suggestions:

- Use the voicemail/answerphone feature properly so that incoming calls don't interrupt intricate tasks. Check regularly, but not more than four times a day.
- Make a timetable for receiving calls and a time when you don't take calls – let clients and colleagues know what this timetable is.
- Set time limits for call backs.
- Plan outgoing calls. What is the objective for the call, what information do you need to have at hand and what actions will arise from the call? Keep a telephone log so that you have a record of what has been said and what actions have to be followed up.
- Start as you mean to go on, a crisp, businesslike approach will call up a similar response. Signal clearly when you are going to end and sum up what has been said and agreed.
- Keep vital telephone numbers in full sight or program them into your phone.

Interruptions

This should not be as much a problem for remote workers as it is for those surrounded by colleagues. However, since most remote workers are targeted not by the amount of time they spend at their desk, but by tasks completed, it is possible to organize things like home deliveries, building work, repairs and such during working hours and make up any time missed outside working hours. Problems may arise, however, if neighbours and friends regard the home worker as constantly available. Many of the remote workers we interviewed said that they had overcome this by setting really firm ground rules when they started working from home (although many of them also said that the worst interrupters were family and not friends).

Junk paperwork

This can build up alarmingly. Time should be put aside to have a regular cull. Most people hoard far too much useless paperwork – just in case. This makes really important paperwork harder to find. Anything that you really cannot bring yourself to throw away should go in a 'rubbish' drawer that is cleared out once a month.

Perfectionism

This is a difficult problem; perfectionists get stressed when forced to act differently. The authors of this book use the phrase 'good enough for military work', which means that there comes a time with any task (particularly things like reports and specifications) when everything has been covered adequately and any more effort is simply polishing.

Crises

First of all work out whether it really is a crisis, and also what the effect of handling the problem immediately will be. If immediate action must be taken, then so be it, but if, for example you would miss an absolutely immovable deadline by leaving what you are doing, then see if there is any way you can defer the crisis until later. Apart from fire, earthquakes, flood and power failures, there are very few business crises that cannot be deferred.

128

Procrastination

Everyone has tasks that they perpetually put off. Prioritizing tasks should help with this. High priority tasks set their own deadlines.

- Break work into do-able chunks – don't try to tackle huge tasks all at once. Make a little project plan for large tasks, breaking them down into phases with measurable progress points. As you pass each point you can build up your motivation by rewarding yourself in some way such as a cup of coffee or a short break. Simply seeing the progress you are making is encouraging in itself.
- Force yourself to make a start (even if it is just for 10 minutes); it is extraordinary how tasks seem easier when you have broken the 'starting tape'.
- And finally – cut off temptation. Switch off the radio or music or hang a DO NOT DISTURB notice on your door. Switch on the answerphone or voice mail, let nothing distract you until you have at the very least done half the task.

Self-Organization

Everyone has their own particular way of working – what might suit someone who finds it easy to tidy up as they go might well be irritating to someone who throws themselves into their work and only tidies up when the paperwork is knee deep in their working space. The important thing is that remote workers feel they are in control of their surroundings and tasks rather than responding reactively. To do this it is helpful when starting out as a remote worker to keep a log of how time has been spent. Keep a simple list of what you do each day and how long each task takes. Also note down any interruptions that happened. Examine this list after a week and decide what work patterns are helpful and what are not. It might be helpful to group certain tasks together. It might be that a worker would be more energized when there are two tasks going on at once, being reinvigorated by changing tasks. Certain tasks might be done more effectively by having a specific time to do them each day (invoicing, report writing etc.). Most people find that having regularly scheduled tasks gives a framework and shape to their working day that disciplines them in the absence of a manager.

Take a look at the times when you feel particularly effective or comfortable with your working practices and ask yourself questions like:

- Do I feel more effective when I have tidied my working space?
- Am I most effective in the morning or afternoon?
- Am I more comfortable when starting tasks than I am when finishing them?
- When are distractions and interruptions at a maximum and a minimum?
- How often do I need to take a break?

Key Points

Try to define when you are most and least comfortable and most and least productive and organize your work patterns accordingly. All the people we interviewed about their working patterns said they very much liked the ability to organize their working day in the way that suited themselves. They also thought that they were much more productive than they would be in an office, and indeed research on remote workers' productivity bears this out.

A word of warning: It is very unhealthy to work at a computer for long stretches without a break. Remote workers who use IT as an integral part of their job need to make sure that they take regular breaks, if necessary using a kitchen timer to remind themselves just how long they have been working. At least once an hour you should stop work, stretch, get up and walk around, take a refreshment break or a short walk. No matter how comfortable your working space, or well organized your desk, slogging away without relaxing from time to time is not good for concentration, accuracy or your health.

Self-Motivation

Many of the remote workers we interviewed told us that they were more often than not motivated by the fact that they were autonomous. Because they could choose how they worked meant that they organized themselves in a way that made their work pleasant and satisfying.

If they had a motivational problem it was usually because they felt they were being ignored or unfairly treated in terms of rewards or career advancement.

This is why it is important that remote workers have a career plan in place. It is all too easy to think only of the day-to-day work that needs to be performed and to ignore the future, particularly if that work is satisfying in itself.

Remote workers should ask themselves the following questions:

- What is the next step in my career?
- Where do I want to be in a year's time?
- What skills will I need in the future and how will I obtain them?
- Do I want to be a remote worker for the rest of my career?
- What opportunities do I have for career development?

Their job appraisal interview is an ideal time for remote workers to discuss these questions with their manager.

Communication Skills

Why Communication Breaks Down

We mentioned in Chapter 4 the importance of clear communication between the manager and the remote worker. One of the difficulties with remote working is that although it is useful and beneficial to have a particular time slot put aside for communication between the manager and the remote worker, this can lead to a tendency to save up information, worries and, particularly, problems or mistakes. This causes several rather unfortunate consequences:

- People forget issues and details.
- The problem gets worse over the intervening time.
- Stress rises with worry.
- Other tasks depending on the remote worker may become delayed.

The answer here is to get help as soon as it is needed and keep details of problems and mistakes in a Day Book so that when the remote worker rings the manager nothing is forgotten. Naturally, most people dislike the idea of seeming inefficient and needing their manager too often, but in the case of the remote worker a stitch in time really will save nine. It is the manager's prime job to help, support and advise the remote worker and unless help is asked for when it is needed, how can the manager possibly know when to intervene? It is a fine balance, but one that needs to be worked out early on in the relationship.

However, with the best will in the world and with all the correct procedures in place communication can still break down. Here are the rules for good communication.

- When communication takes place, people should be able to both hear and see the people with whom they are communicating. They should be near enough to each other to be able to do this. We pick up an enormous amount of information from body language and sub-verbal clues. Sadly the remote worker does a great deal of communication without the advantage of face-to-face contact. They cannot see the body language clues that tell them how someone is responding to what they say and equally the other person is missing the clues that the remote worker is giving out. This means that active listening is vital to the remote worker. Active listening means positive attentiveness, showing that you are listening by using encouraging noises, summarizing what the other person has said and asking for clarification if there is anything unclear.
- When interacting with others, people should stick to the same topics and activities (for example social chit-chat, news seeking and giving, negotiating, interviewing) and should not suddenly change to a different topic or activity.
- Interruptions (unless it is a request for information) break the communication cycle; it is important to listen all the way through any statement before responding.
- Responses should be appropriate and reciprocal. For example, a laugh is an appropriate response to a joke, or a sympathetic comment appropriate to bad news.
- If you want to change the subject, you should signal this clearly.

Written Communication

This is one of the major channels of communication between the remote worker and the office. For this reason written communication should be as efficient as possible. Business communication is not a rambling discussion on a wide and unrelated number of topics (Dear Mum, the cats are well, little Billy has his first tooth and the wallpaper in the bathroom has peeled off again ...) but a set of clear, concise statements that can be digested quickly and filed easily. Stick to one topic per communication.

Don't rush into written communication. It is a time-consuming and expensive activity. Consider whether it is necessary to write or whether there are other methods that would be more efficient. If you need an immediate response or action it might be better to telephone, rather than wait for a response over email or by post.

- To write effectively it is important to plan before starting to write.
- Make sure that the reader knows what the communication is about at the start of the communication.
- Try to make the communication as easy to read and as clear as possible.
- Stick to the point and do not include extraneous information.
- Make sure that all contact information is included and that you name the communication in a way that will allow you to find it again easily, whether in hard copy or electronically.
- Always consider the outcomes of what you have written and ask yourself what needs to be done next.

Considering the amount of mail that people receive each working day, the more concise and business-like it is, the more gratefully it will be received.

Problem Solving and Decision Making

Remote workers have to solve problems and make decisions by themselves significantly more often than office-based workers who have the option of discussion with their colleagues or manager.

This is a series of steps that can be applied to any decision, whether simple or complex:

1. You become aware of a problem, either because it is obvious or because you are picking up clues such as lengthening time scales, deadlines being missed, quality standards dropping or work taking longer than usual.
2. You then need to identify the exact nature of the problem and think about how the solution is to be explained to anyone involved. Unless it is helpful, at this point try not to dwell on past mistakes or blame, but rather look for a way round the problem.
3. Set the rules and time scales. What constraints exist, what health and safety considerations are there? What are the budgets and what resources do you need?
4. Look for alternative solutions. Your first solution may not be the most effective one. Is there anyone else who could help you with this? An outsider's viewpoint can be very effective here.
5. Choose the best solution. What resources will you need to solve the problem? What do you already have? What do you still need? Where will the resources come from?
6. Implement the decision.
7. Provide feedback on the initial problem.

The benefit of using a structured decision making tool is that you make the decision in easily defined stages and have the chance to examine the consequences of your decision before you commit yourself to action. Quite often in business poor decisions are made unnecessarily because stage 2 (recognize and define the problem) is omitted, particularly if only one person seems to be involved. When this happens you miss the opportunity to see how the perceived problem affects others in your team or company. It is always worth remembering that what may be a problem to the remote worker may not be a problem to the company.

Summary

Remote working demands considerable discipline. The primary need is for a structured working environment that will make tasks easier to perform. This is not to say that everything must be strictly regimented, more that the remote worker should really think about what they can personally do to make their job more effective. All the remote workers we interviewed said that they found the supporting tasks that were necessary to their business took up much more time than they thought. Once they had organized a timetable that took this into account they found working life much more comfortable.

9

The Home Office Environment

Once workers are home-based, even if it is only for one day a week, then it follows that they need somewhere at home to work. This chapter outlines the factors that need to be taken into account when converting domestic space for business use. The focus is on 'office' environments, but some consideration is also given to some light engineering activities, such as minor maintenance of electronic equipment and food preparation. No attention has been given to specialist environments, for example for medical staff, who may require tailored facilities for reasons of hygiene etc. These are considered to be outside the scope of this book, and it is assumed that any organization considering such specialist remote working will have the appropriate expertise in-house to specify the appropriate working environment.

Suggestions are given for practical solutions for working in the home environment. The scope of any changes that need to be made will depend upon the amount of time that a remote worker spends at the home base. What is appropriate for someone who spends a few hours a week working at home may not be suitable for another person who spends three or four days a week there.

Converting space in the home will typically be something that the remote worker takes on for him or herself. It is unlikely to be either appropriate or cost-effective for the employer to become financially involved in alterations to an employee's home. However, it is useful to be able to offer advice as to the options available and their suitability.

Employers may well be involved to the extent that they may be providing equipment and related furniture. The employer is well advised to carry out some form of site survey to ensure that the premises are suitable in terms of health and safety, security, working conditions and suitability for housing supplied equipment.

Employers are also advised that they are responsible for the health and safety of remote workers just as they are for office- and factory-based staff. They should make sure that any remote worker has a suitable environment to work in, and that implies costs for inspection.

How Much Space?

How much space is required depends on how much working space the individual worker needs for him or herself and how much equipment is needed in there with them. Another consideration is whether people will come to the location for meetings, and if so how many, and whether samples or stock will need to be stored. Of course, the more space there is the easier life is; it is more pleasant to be able to get up and walk about than it is to be jammed against a wall with only enough room to stand up or sit down. But the reality of incorporating an office into a home that is probably pretty full already means that space will be at something of a premium.

As a starting point it is suggested that one person with a desk, small meeting area, modest storage and filing requirements needs a space that is at least 9 square metres. Figure 5 shows a scale representation of a space using typical dimensions for desk, chair, bookcase and so forth. This has been fitted into about 3 metres by 2 metres (6 square metres). In the language of an estate agent this work would be 'a child's single bedroom'. This leaves no space to move about or have meetings, but it does give an idea of the baseline requirement.

A relatively small increase in the available space, by about an extra metre in either dimension, would allow for a small meeting space big enough for two to three people. When not used for that purpose it provides useful extra working space.

To work in a small office requires a discipline of tidiness that can be relaxed where there is more room to spread out.

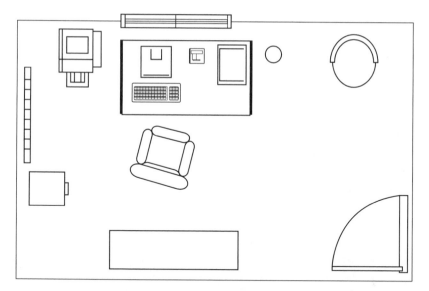

Figure 5

Key Points

A question for the remote worker is, 'Can I work in this space for a whole day?' If the answer is no, then there is little chance of remote working being effective. Of course not all remote workers need to be there all day, in which case the question becomes, 'Can I cope with working there for part of the time?' Again, unless the answer is yes, then remote working will not be effective there.

Working Environment

Given that there is enough space, the next thing to consider is access, power, heat, ventilation, light, plumbing and services. All these, with the possible exception of plumbing, will be needed and if not present will have to be installed. The following notes have been put together to provide some guidance.

Access

This may seem obvious but, as evidenced by people who have constructed a yacht in their back garden and then found that they can't get it out without hiring a crane or a helicopter, access to the home office is important. In most cases this will not be a problem; a standard door big enough for a person to get through will be big enough for the equipment to be used, although furniture may have to be taken to bits to get it into the room. However, this is not the end of the access story. If it is to be used legally as a home office on behalf of an employer, then health and safety regulations may also have to be met in terms of access to and from the office space. Where wheelchair access is needed then ramps and wider doors may be needed. It is worth noting that there are grants available for the conversion of premises where a person has become disabled. In the case that a worker is being offered remote working for reason of disability then these should be investigated.

Key Points

It is unlikely that an organization's employers and public liability insurance will cover use of an employee's home office for client visits.

Access also covers the ability to deliver and collect from the premises, and availability of parking if co-workers or possibly visitors are expected as part of the job. The remote worker will be able to supply this information without the need for a site visit.

The author's know of at least one example where a loft space was converted for home use, but access remained via a ladder. The only way to get even flat-pack office furniture up there was in individual components. This might be no good for company-provided office furniture and certainly would have been unacceptable for visitors – not to mention failing to meet health and safety requirements.

Power

Any worker who is to be home-based will have equipment that requires electric power installed. This will typically be a computer, a printer and a mobile phone, though it may extend to air conditioners, soldering irons, test equipment and, of course, something to make hot drinks. All these will require power, and each will need at least one socket (personal computers often need two, one for the system box and one for the display monitor). When considering a home office space due consideration needs to be given to the number of sockets required (don't forget to have at least one spare socket to plug in the vacuum cleaner; it is too easy to unplug a computer at a critical moment and lose important data).

Key Points

Trailing cables are a sure fire recipe for disaster: at best they get tripped over and pulled out of the socket, at worst they can lead to serious injury. Where they are unavoidable put them in cable protectors that you can walk over safely.

Both the number and the location of the sockets needed must be taken into account when considering the layout and ergonomics of the workspace. If it is not intended to install the large number of power sockets that may be required on a permanent basis, then consider using distribution boxes. These are typically four-way, but also come in two-, three- and six-way, with optional power conditioning to protect the attached equipment from spikes and surges and so forth. These can be conveniently located and fixed to the desk where the equipment is located. Keeping cabling runs to a minimum is the goal here, both for tidiness and for health and safety.

Domestic power supplies may not be the best in the world, and some consideration should be given to power conditioning (filtering out potentially damaging power surges and spikes) if equipment damage is to be avoided. This can be achieved using simple filters that plug in between the computer and the main socket. If some level of power continuity is required, to protect against potential data loss (see also Chapter 7 on Technology) then a so-called 'Un-interruptible Power Supply' (UPS) may be needed. Battery backed-up versions are not expensive and will typically give 10 minutes or so to save work and close down the machine after the main electricity has failed. They often have a facility to do this automatically in the event of such a failure.

Equipment requiring three-phase power is unlikely to be needed by the type of remote workers who are the subject of this book. If there is such a requirement then its availability and the cost of connection will be significant factors in determining suitability of role for a home base.

Key Points

It is a golden rule that you can never have too many power outlets. This is one case where less is definitely not more.

Heat and Ventilation

Health and safety regulations specify acceptable ranges of temperature for a comfortable working environment; at the time of writing in the UK this was between 15 and 25°C for office workers. In modern houses cold is unlikely to be the main problem, however heat often is, particularly in a small space packed with computer equipment. It may be necessary to look at portable air conditioners (which can be rented if only needed in the summer) if there is heat build-up.

Similarly, if someone is going to work effectively they need to have a healthy supply of fresh air. Anyone who doubts this only has to spend a short time in a small meeting room with several people and closed windows and doors to see how everyone quickly drops off to sleep. If a person is going to work at home it will be essential that the room they use, typically a small one, must have suitable ventilation.

The authors were forced to obtain a small portable air conditioner to keep temperatures under control in their own loft conversion. Even in the UK on a moderately warm summer's day the temperature in the loft easily exceeded 30°C.

Light

Lighting is very important for any work. Having the wrong amount/type of lighting will quickly have a negative impact on any worker. A combination of natural and artificial light is preferable to one where only artificial light is available. If detailed or intricate work is required then focused, high intensity, lighting may be needed. As a rule the lighting should be as good as that found in a conventional office or workstation.

Key Points

Don't forget to take into account the seasonal factors when considering lighting – a room that is light enough in the summer and only requires minimal additional lighting in the day time can often require artificial lighting all day long in winter. Similarly, changes in lighting as the sun moves from East to West can be an issue (night and day are taken for granted here).

Communications and Other Services

This includes any other requirements, such as connection to proprietary telephone networks, water and sewerage, cleaning and so on, that are needed for the remote worker to function effectively. As a minimum it will include some form of telecommunications access, though this may be simply a mobile phone. Broadband, either via telephone or cable provider, is desirable, but it is not always available outside of metropolitan areas.

 internet.

Only where food preparation, meeting facilities, and specialist needs are encountered are water, plumbing and sewerage likely to be an issue. In these cases there may be a requirement for additional services relating to maintenance of refrigeration equipment and the like.

Availability of post and delivery services is not normally an issue, but if the location is very remote it may be necessary to consider the frequency of these. For example, if the nearest post collection box is some miles' drive away with only one collection a day and the job role requires use of the mail, then this is probably impractical.

Key Points

Working environments need to be kept clean and tidy. An employer should consider if it is worth making staff an allowance to have their home office cleaned periodically instead of them spending productive time doing it themselves.

Ergonomics

In most home offices space is at a significant premium. Consequently, when setting up a remote working space consideration needs to be given to ergonomics to an even greater degree than is necessary in the conventional work place.

The layout has to be chosen to make the best use of the space available and to make working in that space as easy as possible. The first thing to do is make sure that you can access all the areas, for example desk, chair, filing cabinet, computer, printer and so on. A good way of doing this is to make a two dimensional scale model of the floor plan and the desk, chair, filing cabinet, location of doors, radiators, windows etc. The pieces can then be moved about to get an idea of what is physically possible and what gives the best working space. This is much easier than trying to heave the furniture around in the confines of the room.

There are also computer packages available for both PC and Apple PC systems which make this easier. HR departments, or those implementing remote working, might consider offering the use of such software as part of an induction pack. However, the 'old technology' approach above works perfectly well.

Workstation ergonomics

There are standard guidelines for the use of a computer at a desk. They are summarized below. The source for much of this material was the Health and Safety Executive (HSE) and the latest version of this can be found on their website as (HSE. INDG36(rev1) 5/02 C2250 http://www.hse. gov.uk/). It is available in hard copy as *Display screen equipment work. Health and Safety (Display Screen Equipment) Regulations 1992. Guidance on Regulations* L26 (HSE Books, 1992, ISBN 0 7176 0410 1). There is also a specific guide for employers with a checklist, entitled *VDUs: An easy guide to the regulations HSG90* (HSE Books, 1994, ISBN 0 7176 0735 6). Although this is the booklet HSE recommends for most employers who have staff using standard VDUs in offices it is also relevant for remote workers. It gives practical guidance, in plain language, on how to comply with the Regulations with a minimum of effort and expense. It is illustrated in colour and includes a checklist for workstation assessment.

These guidelines have legal force in the UK for employers whose workforce have to make extensive use of a workstation as part of their job. This is true whether they are home- or office-based. Self-employed people are not usually covered, however if they are working on a client's site then they may come under the same regulations.

The following extracts from these guidelines (© Crown Copyright acknowledged) provide an overview of employers' obligations:

1. Analyse workstations and assess and reduce risks
- employers need to look at: the whole workstation, including equipment, furniture and the work environment
- the job being done; and
- any special needs of individual staff (whose views may be sought as part of the assessment)

Where risks are identified, the employer must take steps to reduce them.

2. Ensure workstations meet minimum requirements
These requirements are good features that should normally be found in a workstation, such as adjustable chairs and suitable lighting. They are set out in a schedule to the Regulations, covering screens, keyboards, desks, chairs, the work environment and software. All workstations covered by the Regulations now have to comply, to the extent necessary for the health and safety of workers (a transitional period for modification of older workstations expired at the end of 1996).

3. Plan work so there are breaks or changes of activity
As the need for breaks depends on the nature and intensity of the work, the Regulations require breaks or changes of activity but do not specify their timing or length. However the guidance on the Regulations explains general principles, for example short, frequent breaks are better than longer, less frequent ones. Ideally the individual should have some discretion over when to take breaks.

4. On request, arrange eye tests and provide spectacles if special ones are needed
Employees covered by the Regulations can ask their employer to provide and pay for an eye and eyesight test. This is a test by an optometrist or doctor. There is also an entitlement to further tests at regular intervals; the optometrist doing the first test can recommend when the next should be. Employers only have to pay for spectacles if special ones (for example, prescribed for the distance at which the screen is viewed) are needed and normal ones cannot be used.

5. Provide health and safety training and information

Employers have to provide training, to make sure employees can use their VDU and workstation safely, and know how to make best use of it to avoid health problems, for example by adjusting the chair. Information should also be provided about VDU health and safety. This should include general background information – this could be done by giving out copies of this booklet. It should also cover more specific details of the steps taken by the employer to comply with the Regulations, such as the action taken to reduce risks and the arrangements for breaks.

Flooring

Practicality is the first consideration when considering the type of flooring to be used in any home working space. It can come as a surprise, particularly to those with pets and children, but office space gets a higher level of wear and tear than domestic accommodation does. This is because considerable activity is concentrated in one place, around a desk and chair, which rapidly results in serious damage to an ordinary domestic carpet. Modern laminate flooring provides a good, and economical, surface. This is attractive, easy to install (and remove) and can be wiped clean.

Pattern of use is the key factor in determining the best solution here. Will the remote worker be at their desk all day long, every day, or will they be out and about visiting clients and only completing minor administration tasks there at the end of the week?

Of course if any kind of equipment or industrial process is envisaged (for example soldering/repair of electronic equipment or light maintenance work) that has requirements over and above those of an office environment then suitable flooring will be required. Food preparation will also add specific requirements in terms of being washable and resistant to hygiene products.

One of the authors works in a converted loft space. The main floor in this loft consists of flooring boards painted with cream floor paint plus some rugs. It rapidly became apparent that, whilst this was fine for general light use as envisaged by the builder, the area around the desk would rapidly become ruined by the office chair.

The solution was to install a small rectangular area of laminate flooring to take the desk and the chair. This provided a cheap and removable, hard wearing surface that protects the floor beneath for future use.

Decoration

This should be appropriate for the work that is to be done there, whilst taking into consideration any requirements for dual use. Unless client meetings are to be held at the remote worker's base then this is not such an issue as flooring – the only person who will need to look at it will be the home worker and wear and tear is not an issue. However, it should be as practical as possible. Give consideration to ease of cleaning and repair. Surfaces should be easy to wipe clean and match in colour in case of damage (have a look round a typical office – it gets more minor bumps than you might think).

Where meetings are likely to be held at the remote site then a neutral décor is the best starting point. It can be distracting to have a meeting in a converted nursery room that still has fluffy bunnies romping over the walls. Consideration should also be given to the ease with which the space can be converted back to domestic use. Again, a neutral colour scheme will help here.

In the case of activities that have special hygiene requirements then this will impact the materials that can be used for decoration in the same way that it may affect the choice of flooring.

[*Note:* On the whole the authors do not recommend that remote worker's premises be used for customer meetings and that even internal meetings should be kept to a minimum. In general it is not likely to give a good impression, and it can cause problems with regulations relating to domestic use. It can also lead to problems with neighbours relating to parking and so on.]

Conversions

When looking for suitable space for remote working in the home and there is no immediate space suitable, then converting an existing space should be considered. This can range in expense from the trivial to the

significant. For the self-employed this then becomes a personal investment decision, for the employer/employee things are more complex.

*A remote worker was made redundant about 6 months after being
provided with desk, chair, filing cabinet, notebook PC, printer and
other related equipment. The computer equipment was returned to
the employer, but the desk, chair, filing cabinet and minor items were
given to the ex-employee rather than incur cost of collection and as a
gesture of good will. This was reasonable, but if a significant
investment had been made in converting, for example, a garage then
the issue would have been more complex. Most employers will not
fund expensive conversions.*

The following points are provided to give an insight into what is involved
in typical conversions and their pros and cons. The extent of many will
put them out of bounds for employers.

Rooms

If there is a spare bedroom, utility space, or the flat or house already has
a room that is not in full time use for another purpose then this is the
first location that will typically be considered for a home base for the
remote worker.

The advantages are obvious – there will be light, power and the basic
structure to support the office and its equipment already in place.
Furthermore, the space will probably have its own door and that can be
closed and the working area separated from the rest of the home. It can
be as easy as just adding some furniture and a communications line.

Often when considering converting a room for use by a remote worker
it has to be considered that the end result will need to be dual use – by
day as a work place then in the evening for use by the whole household.

■ **Advantages**
- Usually very cheap to implement.
- Can easily be used for other purposes if remote working ceases.
- Usually no requirements for planning permission/building
  regulations.

■ **Disadvantages**
- Can intrude on day-to-day running of the home.
- May need to be used for other purposes than an office.
- May detract from value.
- In rented property landlord may forbid such use.
- Leasehold property may also have restrictions.
- If expenses claimed, can have tax implications.

Lofts

This will depend very much on the nature of the building. Modern construction often does not lend itself to the conversion of a loft space into an additional room; older properties tend to be better, but it is a major job if there is no existing staircase. A loft ladder is not a practical means of access. That said, if a loft conversion is possible then it makes an ideal business space, as it is effectively separate from the main part of the house. It is possible to 'go to work' in a way that does not affect the smooth running of the rest of the house.

Excessive heat in the summer is a common problem with lofts. Even with the British summer the authors have had to install a portable air conditioner to keep temperatures down to those that are comfortable for both people and equipment to work in.

■ **Advantages**
- Easily separated from rest of home.
- Adds value to property.
- Often inexpensive.
- Can easily be used for other purposes if remote working ceases.

■ **Disadvantages**
- Heating/cooling may be a problem.
- Access stairs may be inconvenient.
- Building regulation approval usually needed.
- Planning permission may be needed.
- Fire escape facilities may be required.
- If expenses claimed, can have tax implications.

Garages

For those who have no space available to sacrifice in their own home, letting the car get wet is one of the first options to consider. A single-car garage will provide more than adequate space for the average remote worker, indeed at a minimum size of 4 metres by 6 metres there is room for both an office and a meeting area – even spare space for an extra desk. It may even be possible to partition off part of the garage, leaving the rest suitable for use by a small car. However, most garages, even those integral to the house, are fairly basic. Electrical power may be present for lighting, but the floor will typically be rough concrete, the walls bare breeze blocks or brick and the main door anything but draught free. It will be too cold in winter and too hot in summer unless something is done to bring the standard up to that of the domestic accommodation.

- **Advantages**
  - Easily separated from rest of home.
  - May provide very generous accommodation.
  - Inexpensive to convert if structure sound.
  - Can be reconverted if required.
- **Disadvantages**
  - May require building regulation/planning permission.
  - If there is no external driveway (as in some town houses), may cause car to be kept on street.
  - Insulation is often poor so heating and cooling may be expensive and non-recoverable in terms of cost.

Sheds/Outbuildings/Gazebos/Caravans etc.

One of the benefits of using an outside space, if the remote worker is lucky enough to have it, is that work can be totally separated from the home. This can be very useful where family life is likely to be intrusive. The remote worker literally goes to the office as does any site-based employee – the office just happens to be in the garden. Many people like to have this delineation between home and work so this can be a popular solution.

As with garages, outbuildings can be fairly basic in their raw state. They are typically temporary structures, so often require no planning permission. What is suitable for keeping a lawn mower happy and occasional woodwork use is going to fall a long way short of what is needed for useable office space.

- **Advantages**
  - Easily separated from rest of home.
  - Self-contained space that can be dedicated to office use.
  - Does not impact on rest of the home.
  - Often exempt from planning permission.
- **Disadvantages**
  - May require power to be supplied via underground cables etc.
  - Unlikely to be well insulated, may be damp etc. so can be expensive.
  - May require additional insurance/may not be insurable.
  - Physical security may be a problem.
  - If expenses claimed, can have tax implications.

Some people have even been known to use locally moored narrow boats as offices, and in at least one case, a tree house.

Small Spaces

Included in this category are spaces under the stairs, alcoves, former lavatories, closets, large cupboards, box rooms and the like. Effectively anything where the space is limited to about the size of an ordinary office desk come into this category.

- **Advantages**
  - Does not need to significantly reduce accommodation available in the rest of the home.
  - Unlikely to require planning permission/building regulations approval.
  - Typically inexpensive.
  - Unlikely to have property tax issues.
  - Easily reversible if remote working ceases.
- **Disadvantages**
  - Cramped working areas are not good if used for more than occasional use.

- Lack of storage space may be a problem.
- May not be separate from the main body of the home, so not quiet when needed.
- Ventilation/cooling may be an issue.

Extensions

Although it is often feasible to build on to a property, this is likely to be an expensive option for either the employer or the remote worker and represents a long-term investment.

■ **Advantages**
- Custom design gives the opportunity to create an excellent working environment.
- May be self-financing in the long term if it adds value to the property (see also disadvantages).
- Easily funded by mortgage.

■ **Disadvantages**
- Typically major projects and therefore very expensive for the remote worker.
- Usually only practical for workers who own their own property.
- Planning and building regulation requirements can lead to long lead times before the space is available for use.
- May not add to the value of the property by as much as the project costs.
- Often too expensive an investment for an employer.

Key Points

An employer needs to make sure that any proposed base for home working is suitable for use. An inspection visit will be needed and this is a cost that needs to be taken into consideration.

Regulations

In the United Kingdom there can be both planning and building regulations to be considered when converting part of a property for office use. In this chapter we have tried to suggest where these are more/less likely to be needed. If in any doubt a suitably qualified expert should be consulted.

In addition, there may be restrictions placed by landlords, terms of a lease, local bye-laws, and so forth that relate to changes to use/modifications to the property. If in any doubt, make enquiries. It is the case that many housing associations and providers of social housing have specific regulations discouraging home working. When assessing staff for suitability for home working, identifying any insurmountable regulations should be done as early as possible both to save time and to avoid setting undeliverable expectations.

The nature of the work needs to be considered in terms of the neighbourhood too. Because they make no impact on local facilities no one will be bothered by someone working at home and indoors. However, if they have a string of visitors, perhaps creating parking problems, there may be issues. Not only can this lead to friction with neighbours it can also lead to formal complaints to the local council or planning authority.

There are also tax implications for home office space. These depend on what expenses are claimed against the use of the property. It is important that remote workers are provided with advice on the implications of any changes they make in terms of potential capital gains, council tax and inland revenue regulations. Remote workers must be made fully aware of what these tax/financial regulations are (and these change with time and so need to be monitored) and advised of the consequences of any action they take. There must be no financial surprises to the remote worker that result from decisions they make at the behest of their employer.

[*Note*: By and large there should be no problems in working part-, or full-time in a person's own home. However, it is very important to make sure before making changes, even if this only involves warning neighbours of the delivery of office equipment.]

Who Pays?

This is a fundamental consideration. In the case of the self-employed or freelance worker the answer is simple – they do. This can be funded in a number of ways, for example by a mortgage, a bank loan, or in cases where the price is low, from the cash flow of the business. The expenses may be set against tax, though it is important to check on the overall tax position when doing this as it can generate liability for capital gains tax when the home is sold or incur business rates. These can easily offset any benefits from claiming the expenses against tax.

For the employed the answer is much more complex. For example, provision of a computer, a communications line, mobile phone and so forth is still straightforward, the employer accepts installation, removal and rental costs as part of normal operations. However, if conversion costs are likely to add value to the remote worker's property, then the issue is less clear-cut. For most organizations this will rule such investments out. Where significant investment is made in the employee's home there should be a well-documented, and mutually understood, agreement on what happens if the remote worker either returns to on-site based working or leaves the organization.

As with the case of the self-employed, if an employee is given an allowance for using part of their home for business, or claims allowances against tax and so forth then it may affect the status of the home. It is important that this is sorted out before remote working is committed to.

One of the organizations we reviewed had a strict policy of 'we need to own everything used by the employee' for equipment, including desks and chairs. This solved many administrative and health and safety, intellectual copyright, Data Protection Act, insurance and other problems, and in our view is the best starting point when looking at remote working.

Insurance

The insurance (for fire, theft, accidental damage etc.) that most owner-occupiers have for their own home will usually include cover for the owner working at home, though this should be checked. It is less likely to cover working at home where there are frequent visitors, public access or specialist activities including food preparation and the use of certain equipment. However it is unlikely to cover property that is not owned by the occupier. In the case of tenants/housing associations the situation will be more complex as it will involve both the employee's and the landlord's insurance policies.

Similarly, an organization's insurance for equipment used by employees may include cover for use away from organization premises. Again, there are often restrictions on this limiting the cover to, for example, theft only.

Consequently it is dangerous to assume that the combination of the existing cover of the organization and that of the employee will overlap to meet all eventualities. Indeed, it is most unlikely that it will, and so an investigation into what is, and is not covered needs to be made and an assessment made of the cost of any additional cover versus the risk/impact of the event if no cover exists. Insurance should cover both the remote worker and the sponsoring organization.

Some conversions, for example of a temporary structure such as a garden shed, may not be insurable and this should be established before work takes place.

Another, perhaps more critical, insurance issue relates to employer's and public liability insurance. Self-employed people and contract workers with their own limited company are likely to have their own insurance which covers them, and visitors, for accidents that might happen whilst visitors are on their premises. It is unlikely that an organization's standard insurance policies cover will extend to home-based offices. Consequently meetings involving non-organization staff should not be held at these premises.

Key Points

Check out insurance requirements before committing to any use of a remote site. Do not encourage business visitors unless you are sure they are adequately insured.

Health and Safety

It is tempting to think that having a home-based workforce will save the employer from the overhead of health and safety. However, as already touched upon in some of the sections of this chapter, health and safety rules apply to the employers of remote-based staff in much the same way as if they were on the company site. In addition, they apply to many subcontracted self-employed workers too. Health and safety is an important issue for any organization implementing remote working and is a major cost driver. Any HR/Personnel department involved in implementing remote working needs to expand its existing H&S policies and practices to include the remote sites.

Key Points

The Health and Safety at Work etc. Act places duties on employers, self-employed people and employees. Under this, employers have a duty to protect the health, safety and welfare of their employees, including home-based workers. Most of the Regulations made under the act apply equally to employees working at an organization's workplace and to home/remote-based workers. These include, but are not limited to, the Management of Health and Safety at Work Regulations, the Manual Handling Operations Regulations, the Display Screen Equipment Regulations, the Provision and Use of Work Equipment Regulations and the Control of Substances Hazardous to Health Regulations (COSHH).

In addition, if remote premises are being used for any industrial processes (for example repair of electrical equipment or food preparation), then the regulations will usually be the same as for a commercial site. This may result in significant expense/difficulties.

Essential elements of H&S for remote workers include: audit; inspection; on-site equipment; training and awareness. In some cases there may be a specific COSHH requirement.

Key Points

H&S processes need to keep a sensible balance between minimizing risk and obeying regulations without making productive work impossible. You can make a car very safe by welding the doors shut, removing the engine and not allowing anyone within a hundred yards of it. However, this does rather remove the point of having a car!

Audit

Once it has been determined where the remote worker is based then a health and safety audit of the premises should be carried out. The details of this will vary with the current legislation and the H&S polices of the organization, the nature of the work and the equipment involved. However, the principal areas of inspection will include:

1. Access
2. Fire escapes and extinguishers/procedures
3. Cabling and obstructions
4. Seating and working spaces
5. Suitability of flooring/surface decorations
6. Ventilation, heating and cooling
7. Lighting
8. Hygiene
9. First aid
10. COSHH requirements

[*Note:* In the case of conversions the audit needs to be completed once the work is finished.]

Repeat Inspections

It is not enough to get things right once. The audit will ensure that all necessary regulations have been obeyed and that good practice is established. However, unless there is some form of monitoring process then there is nothing to ensure that this continues to be the case. Consequently repeat inspections are needed. It may be practical for these to be done by the remote worker him or herself using a checklist. However, proper records should be kept and it is desirable (in some cases it may even be a legal requirement, check this) that some third party inspections be carried out from time to time.

On-site Equipment

Any H&S related information that is required for any on-site equipment needs to be made available to the remote worker and provision needs to be made for the worker to access it easily from the remote site. For example, a filing cabinet may be too heavy for one person to lift safely, in which case provision needs to be made to provide assistance should it need to be moved. Fire extinguishers may be required, and the correct types will need to be identified depending on the type of equipment installed at the premises.

Hygiene

For a remote worker in his or her own home this should not be an issue for the employer unless they are supplying food to be consumed there, or the role involves food preparation/similar. However, if meetings are likely to be held at these premises then there are rules governing washroom facilities, refrigerators, food and drink preparation areas and related activities. As before, we direct the reader to the relevant HSE websites.

[*Note*: If a remote site is used for catering then it will need to conform to all the appropriate regulations as if it were a commercial site. It will open to inspection in the same by the usual authorities.]

Training and Promotion

H&S procedures only work if the people involved receive relevant training and are sold the benefits of the concept. Keeping training sensible, relevant and not overly restrictive wherever possible will make acceptance of the procedures that much more likely. Where possible the training should be directly relevant to the main tasks of the remote worker concerned. It is also the authors' experience that practical training, such as being shown how to tackle a fire in a waste paper bin, has a stronger impact than a lecture on not disposing of cigarette ends in the waste bin! Keep in mind that the remote worker may have to lose more working time to come to a central site for training than a worker already based on that site. Scheduling any training to fit in with another trip to site will be beneficial.

Promotion is also important as H&S has an image of combining the 'nanny state' with obstructive working practices. The solution to this is to only implement policies and regulations in a practical way, with the minimum interference to the way people work. This approach should then be coupled with selling the benefits of the H&S regulations, for example avoiding repetitive strain injuries, to the remote workers.

One of the authors received an H&S induction at a client's site that was very effective because it only covered elements of policy that were directly relevant to the job in hand.

First Aid

Because remote sites typically have only one person working on them there is no legal requirement (at the time of writing) for any first aid provision, or for that matter a requirement for a fire warden. However, it would make sense to review any equipment on site that might be likely to cause injury and consider providing suitable first aid equipment for home use.

COSHH

Care Of Substances Hazardous to Health is a subject in its own right and the HSE website (http://www.hse.gov.uk) carries up-to-date guidance on this. Although unlikely to be a major issue for most remote workers where the most common problems will relate to toner and inkjet printer cartridges and their disposal, COSHH may be a concern. In the case where food preparation is involved then there will certainly be bleaches, disinfectants and the like that will require appropriate storage and labelling.

Key Points

In conventional office premises there is a requirement for various health and safety and insurance related signs and other posters to be displayed. Those implementing remote working should consider both the legal requirement for signage and what may be useful in addition to keep the remote premises safe.

Induction Process

Finally, when researching this book it became clear to us that successful H&S implementations had an induction process that introduced both the concepts and the practice of H&S to staff. It is strongly recommended that a suitable induction process be developed for the remote worker. This may be based upon an existing process, but will be tailored to the needs of those not based on organization premises.

Security

Introduction

Industrial espionage, terrorism, hacker attacks, theft, vandalism, and unauthorized usage are all part and parcel of running any modern organization. Every company should have procedures and resources in place to reduce the risk from these to acceptable levels, irrespective of whether or not they have remote workers. In a conventional organization there will be a limited number of premises to protect and support when implementing the appropriate level of security. With remote working the numbers of premises is greatly increased and more complex to look after. This short section deals with the major points to be considered and suggests some strategies that might be considered for a remote working implementation in a typical organization. It is the security required while allowing the organization to continue operating.

This section gives an overview of developing security procedures and highlights special factors that come as a result of operating with remote workers. High security operations, such as the security services themselves, sensitive research and development centres, financial and personal data handling will require a more sophisticated approach and the reader should consult with specialist publications and organizations here. A short list is given as a starting point within the bibliography.

Security Areas

When considering security for an organization there are key areas that need to be considered. Table 9.1 lists the main ones that apply. Note that these will be the same for remote and conventional working.

Key Points

When considering security it is important to have a policy that includes all areas of potential risk to the organization and have practical processes to deal with them appropriately. Part of this involves having security processes that have costs commensurate with the value of the information.

Table 9.1 Security areas

Area	Items to consider
Physical	Premises, infrastructure, environment, health and safety
Technology	Equipment, infrastructure, data protection, service continuity
People	Employees, visitors, general public, competitors, terrorists, ex-employees
Disasters	Fire, flood, environmental, health and safety
Business continuity	How will the remote worker continue to work in the event of major disasters at the remote site?

Policy

Developing a security policy for home working is the same as for any other component of an organization, and for an existing organization will simply be a matter of reviewing existing policies and procedures in terms of the impact of having off-site workers, equipment and communications and so forth.

Something like this has happened to many organizations in the past, and will doubtless happen again in the future. A computer, printer and supporting equipment was shipped to a remote worker's site by a shipping agent. Because nobody had checked to make sure there would be a responsible person to receive the equipment the shipper had no one to deliver it to. Consequently they left it, 'out of sight' by a garden shed. Sadly this was witnessed and the equipment was not there when the remote worker returned home.

Summary

Use this checklist as a sanity test before you commit someone, or are committed yourself, to remote working. If you are not sure of any of the answers to these questions, or you are sure but know that what is required has not been provided for, then think carefully before starting remote working.

Question	Checked
Physical environment	
Is there enough physical space available at the remote location?	
Is special security needed?	
Will it meet any applicable health and safety regulations?	
Is access acceptable?	
Are power, heat, light etc. adequately supplied?	
Equipment	
Are power supplies suitable, do they need filtering, UPS?	
Is special power required (e.g. three phase)?	
Family	
What will be the impact of remote working on the family of the remote worker?	
Insurance	
Is the proposed working environment insurable?	
Health and safety	
Policy?	
Audit?	
Repeat inspections?	
Training and PR?	
Hygiene?	
COSHH?	
Induction process?	
Conversions	
Is planning permission required?	
Is building regulation approval required?	
Is power available?	

10

The Remote Worker's Children, Relatives and Pets

It cannot be stressed too highly that remote working is *not* a replacement for proper childcare facilities and appropriate family-friendly procedures. However, one of the benefits of flexible and remote working can be better work–life balance for those with children/dependants. A consequence of this is that the remote workers often find themselves having to work in the same environment, even share their office, with their children/pets and other dependants. This is a factor which is largely out of the control of the employer, but is something on which they should be prepared to offer advice and support. This is not a subject that office-based HR staff and managers will necessarily be familiar with. On the whole it should not be a problem, after all one of the benefits to remote workers is the freedom to fit home and work life together more easily. This chapter offers suggested approaches to the issues that remote workers will encounter that they will not meet up with in the conventional workplace. We have written this chapter in an easy, accessible style with the remote worker in mind, and HR may consider providing those thinking about the change to remote working with a copy to read.

Key Points

Employers should not think that remote workers would suffer more distractions than their office-based counterparts. In many cases it can be much quicker for someone to deal with, for example, a childcare problem if they are on the spot than it is for them to do so from the office.

Children

These are first and foremost the most significant consideration to take into account for remote workers. As stated, organizations should not look on remote/home-based working as a solution for childcare problems. If people are home-based then they will have to spend just as much time concentrating on working as if they are based in an office. They do not have spare time for looking after the children as well.

Key Points

Neither the employer nor the worker should ever confuse remote or home-based working with a solution to childcare provision. You can't get a full day's work done if you are also looking after a six-month-old baby. Increased flexibility is a great help, but it does not change the amount of work that needs to be done in bringing up a child.

We have addressed the needs of pre-school and school age children separately as they are significantly different from a working day point of view.

Pre-school (0–4 or 5 years)

Very young children are demanding and require constant attention and monitoring and it can be considered an offence if they are left on their own, thus putting them at risk (as is the case with all children up to the age of about 13). When they are very young it can be almost impossible to explain the concept that although you are at home, you are not free to play or entertain them at a moment's whim. For this reason, home-based workers will need to make the same level of care provision as do office-based workers.

This provision can take place in the home, or outside the home at a playgroup or a crèche or similar service provider. Either way the care will need to be provided by a third party. It may be cheaper to have this take place in the home, however this then means that the parent is open to higher levels of distraction. As stated it is very difficult to explain to a small child that the parent is not available to play when he or she is clearly visible sitting there at what looks like a television screen. For this reason it is recommended that the external option is taken – even if this is only for part of the day.

Whatever arrangements are made, the key to making it work will be a combination of great time management and having contingency plans to cover all eventualities.

Golden rules:

- Make sure you have sufficient care provision available and in place before you start remote working.
- If possible have this provision away from home, at least for part of the day so that you have some work 'quality' time.
- If you have a nanny or a carer who either lives in or visits your home make sure they understand that you are working and not available to solve their every problem.
- If you are not going to be available at fixed times, e.g. when delivering children to/from childminder then let people know this and set their expectation that they can leave a voice message/email and that you will deal with them promptly on your return.
- Have a plan for dealing with emergencies (for example if the school calls about an accident/illness). This is really the same as it would be for an office-based worker, only it should be easier to arrange as there is no mad dash for home needed.

Prevent access to organization equipment, physically if possible.

Key Points

Most people with small children will be familiar with the effect of a jam sandwich on a video recorder. Be assured that the effect on a printer's paper feed can be even more expensive to cure. Tiny tots and computer equipment do not mix well.

School Age (5–18)

Children in this age range will have the benefit (to the worker) of being away at school during term times. It is quite practical for a remote worker to arrange collection or delivery to school either themselves, or in cooperation with other parents (the infamous 'school run'). The age range has been extended here to 18, although it is perfectly legal to leave 'children' over 16 to their own devices and ignore them if you wish, although in most cases their needs still need to be taken into account.

While they are at school there is less of a problem – the situation is the same as for a solo remote worker. However, it will be necessary to make arrangements to get them to and from school and provide cover for the periods before and after school that are still within working hours. Mobile phones, email and voice mail will minimize the impact of these interruptions to the working schedule, and provided the remote worker sets the expectations of clients and co-workers there should be no insurmountable problems that result from these breaks in the working day.

When it is not school time then to a large extent the situation is similar to that for pre-school children – you need to have suitable provision to look after them whilst you work. A starting point is to work out what you would have done if you were not remote working. Any solution that works in that situation should work when you are at home or another remote site.

Once children are older and can be reasoned with (assuming that this is ever the case!) then it may be practical to agree times when you cannot be disturbed but are still on hand to deal with real emergencies. For example, the authors found this case note on an American teleworking forum. The remote worker was a male computer programmer with a 5-year-old child. He negotiated a deal with his son whereby he would be available to play for the first ten minutes in every hour during the time he was not at school (in working hours). In exchange the son was allowed to choose the activity he wanted to play at. It is reported that this worked well, and though it would be naive to expect that this one negotiation was once and for all, but the principle is sound.

Key Points

It is reasonable to spend the time you would normally spend at the office in breaks for coffee, meals and so forth with your children, relatives, or dependants. It is not a case that they have to be entirely excluded from 9 to 5, but there have to be clear boundaries.

Children of adolescent age and above bring their own problems, but may be open to reason as described above. However, they are likely to be noisier and more liable to mood swings when at home and have more demanding friends. Clear ground rules will be needed unless you are fortunate enough to be able to have sufficient space to escape interruptions. One particularly imaginative solution was to give a 16-year-old male a caravan in the garden to live in. This meant that loud music, smelly socks and mess were not an issue in the main residence (and consequently the home office). At the same time the location of the offspring was known and he was on hand for feeding and washing facilities as required. Of course the office could have been located in the caravan, but this would not have been as advantageous overall.

Another issue with children relates to the use of the organization's equipment. For many reasons (such as viruses, potential breach of confidence etc.) it is usually unacceptable for them to have access to computer, Internet, email or mobile phone equipment. It will often be a disciplinary offence to permit this to happen (if it is not, then HR may like to consider making it one). That this equipment is off limits is an important rule. It is good practice to set such equipment up with passwords that are not made known to any non-organization staff.

Try to follow these **Golden Rules**:

- Make sure you have sufficient care provision available and in place before you start remote working.
- If you are not going to be available at fixed times, e.g. when delivering children to/from school/childminder, then let people know this and set their expectation that they can leave a voice message/email and that you will deal with them promptly on your return.
- Agree quiet times with older children (unless you have a soundproof room for them or you).
- Agree that they should not have friends round after school unless it can be arranged so they don't interrupt you – children cannot be expected to have the self discipline to always be quiet when playing.
- Make it clear that organization equipment (e.g. PC) is off limits and protect with passwords.
- Negotiate fair and readily understood deals with children concerning working time versus 'quality' time with them.
- If you can't make the domestic situation suitable for remote working, then be honest about it and don't do it.

> ### Key Points
>
> One of the reasons that remote and home-based workers need good time management skills is so that they can deal effectively with domestic tasks and distractions without it impacting their ability to deliver.

Adults

Partners and Spouses

By and large these should be no more of a problem, other than with any personal issues, for remote workers than they are for office-based staff. However, where the partner is not working, or also is a home-based worker, then it is important to be sure that working ground rules have been established. These need to cover any issues that might interfere with working duties. The author's have direct experience of this as they used to have adjoining offices with an open connecting door. This led to difficulties when one person had an idea and wanted to discuss it whilst the other was concentrating on writing a training manual. This was not a recipe for smooth working and a deal had to be negotiated around interruptions (when they could/could not be made). This would be even more of an issue if both home workers needed to share the same space.

As with children, access to the organization's equipment should be restricted – again the analogy is with equipment that would normally be located at organization premises.

For partners, these are the **Golden Rules:**

- Agree working times/non working times – it is OK to meet for lunch, even in your own home.
- Define boundaries on access to information/equipment and agree them.
- Set times of the day when you need to be totally quiet if the home is not large enough for a suitably large physical separation.
- Ask them not to answer your business line or sign for deliveries that are for the organization.

- Agree a protocol for interrupting, e.g. knocking on the office door rather than just walking in, at specific break times or similar.
- If they are to have visitors during your working times agree a way of doing this that ensures you are not disturbed.

Key Points

Adults can be just as disruptive as small children, particularly if they do not appreciate the distinction between working and non-working time. In a domestic situation failure to get this established can lead to serious disagreements.

Other Relatives/Dependants

As before, from the employer's point of view the key factor is that these do not prevent the remote worker from being able to deliver their work in a timely manner. The basics are the same as for spouses and children and come down to agreeing that, although you may be physically present, you are working and cannot be disturbed at the drop of a hat. Hopefully it is easier to negotiate ground rules with adult relatives and dependants, though this is by no means guaranteed.

In the case of elderly relatives who need care, then the situation is closer to that of a pre-school child, if only to the extent that you need to make provision for somebody else to take them to day centres, the doctors and so on if it would otherwise interfere with getting the work completed on time.

Privacy

The home situation of the remote worker will be a consideration when setting up support for them or when determining whether home-based working will be suitable. A part of this will be assessing if there is sufficient privacy available for the remote worker to do the job without compromising themselves or those who share the location.

This privacy also needs to extend to the organization itself. It needs to be agreed with all those who have access to the home office that the organization's intellectual property is sacrosanct. The point can be made that if the work was being done in the organization's office then the information would not be accessible to non-organization staff. Just because it is in the home does not mean it is free to all.

Key Points

It is not right for the employer to pry into people's domestic arrangements, but it is useful to be able to offer support where it is asked for. When assessing staff members for their suitability for remote work it is reasonable to ask if there are any factors that might need to be handled when home-based. However, this should be with a view to helping, not interfering.

Security

Although this has been addressed in the sections of the book dealing with technology and policies and procedures, it should be kept in mind that the people who share the remote working environment are a potential risk to information security. Indeed it is quite common for people in the same household to work for competing organizations. Consequently there need to be adequate safeguards, such as access control, to ensure that confidential and sensitive information is kept secure. It is worth noting that, in the case of the Data Protection Act, failures on this front can have expensive consequences.

However, it is important not to get too concerned about this. The fundamental situation is no different than for office-based staff who share accommodation with competitors' employees. The difference is that there is more opportunity for the information to go astray. The security policy needs to cover access control to information, physical security of the premises and who will have physical access at the remote site. This will come down to a risk assessment exercise. In most cases there is no problem, it will only be an issue where sensitive competitive, or security information is involved. In such cases it may be the case that remote working is not appropriate.

Pets

Much less likely to be an issue, but still worth considering are the problems that can come from pets. There are myriad ways that domestic creatures can interfere with the contents of an office – some of which may injure the pet.

Rabbits, rats, mice and other rodents have been known to gnaw through cables with serious results. Parrots have been known to amuse themselves dissecting floppy discs and pulling the keys off keyboards. The working environment needs to be protected from damage by pets and that this can be done should be checked prior to installing expensive equipment.

In terms of the working relationships, remote workers need to make sure that their pets do not interfere with the time available for work. Most organizations would not encourage, or allow, people to bring their pets in to work, so it is reasonable to suggest that pets be kept in check during working hours.

In the case of caged birds, fish and anything else that is not free to roam about there are not likely to be any problems and regular care can be accommodated within the normal daily schedule. Dogs will need some exercise, but again this can be scheduled to fit in with work. Adult cats should be no problem either, though it may be necessary to keep them away from keyboards when in use.

Kittens and Puppies

What goes for tiny children goes double for kittens and puppies. The author's own experience is that it is almost impossible to work when a kitten decides it is playtime. There is no solution for this other than to wait until the kitten/puppy thinks it is time to take a nap or to keep the offender out of the working space and provided with toys/food and access to litter trays as needed. Remote workers should be advised that this is a problem they must solve effectively, even if it means working on site more whilst the kitten/puppy is at its most distracting (subject to suitable care being available for the pet). For the authors this is not such a problem, as being self-employed they can choose work/play time to suit themselves provided they still meet client deadlines.

As mentioned earlier, the destructive powers of small animals if left unattended can be impressive – make sure that puppies and kittens are not left open to the temptation to play with home equipment. Computer mice can suffer the same fate as the real thing.

[*Note*: Part of this book was actually written with a kitten on the desk – productivity was significantly reduced, though not totally eliminated.]

Illness

There are two aspects to sickness when remote working. The first applies to the remote worker; the second applies to those they share their home with.

Remote workers should be encouraged to adopt the same attitude to sickness that office-based staff should. They should not work when they are sick. Apart from humanitarian concerns two factors come to bear: people recover faster if they rest; and they make more mistakes when they work whilst they are ill. Both literature surveys and the authors' own interviews show that remote staff are more likely to work on when sick – at first sight this seems a good thing, but for the reasons described it should not really be encouraged.

In the case of sick relatives then matters are more complicated. The remote worker should inform the manager and let them know if the situation requires them to alter their schedule. This would be the case if they were office-based. The parallel is with childcare – remote working is not an alternative to making proper arrangements, but it does offer scope for flexibility as long as everyone involved is kept up to date with the current situation. Effective communication is the key factor.

Summary

For both people and pets the important thing is to make sure that they are integrated into the routine of the remote worker in a way that allows both to function effectively. From the employer's point of view it is essential that appropriate controls are put in place to make sure that equipment and information is not put at risk. It is also important to offer support to employees who find difficulty in coping with the demands of those with whom they share the remote working environment.

The remote worker needs to come up with workable strategies and techniques for dealing with people and pets that share what is effectively their working environment. If they don't, then this will become rapidly apparent to both themselves and the employer (or client) and the working relationship will be in great danger of failing. That said, when it is made to work then society, the organization and the individual all benefit.

11

Risk and Remote Working

A good way of summarizing all the things that need to be put in place in order to implement an effective and successful remote working system is to look at the risks associated with it. This book is not about risk management as such (readers wishing to know more are referred to our *Managing Projects* or to any of the relevant books listed in the bibliography) but here we do offer a very short description of risk management. It is recommended that anyone implementing remote working should complete their own risk management exercise, both from the point of view of the employer and the employee before setting out. The risks identified, and possible risk plans outlined here, should be seen as a starting point upon which to build a customized plan for implementing remote working within the target organization.

Risk Management

Figure 6 shows a classic approach to risk management. It is typical of that used in formal methodologies such as PRINCE 2 (see Glossary). It consists of a continuous cycle of identification, assessment, planning and monitoring that carries on until the implementation is finished. For a remote working implementation this means it carries on until remote working ceases. This cycle works for any industry or market sector, it is simple and well established. The descriptions that follow are minimalist and are only intended to ensure that the non-specialist reader can understand the sample risk table that makes up the real information content of this chapter.

Figure 6

Identification and Assessment

These stages are combined here for convenience; in practice the assessment is often a separate exercise that is carried out by a suitably qualified team once all the risks have been identified. However, here we are assuming that an initial assessment will be made when each risk is identified. Risks are identified by consulting with/interviewing those involved in the implementation of remote working. Typically this would include human resources, management, employees and technical/ specialist staff.

Risk # R0001	*Severity High* *High/Medium/Low*	*Probability Low* *High/Medium/Low*	*Date dd/mm/yy*
Description *Change in health and safety legislation leads to excessive cost of implementation in domestic properties. Would require weekly inspection visits to every remote site with full written report copied to central file and available for audit by H&S executive on demand.*			
Interviewer: *David Nickson*		Interviewee: *Suzy Siddons*	

[*Note*: It may well be the case that some risks are sufficiently similar to be merged with others.]

Prioritization

Once all the risks have been identified the next step is to ignore those that can be considered realistically not to affect the project. For example, all low probability risks might be ignored when paired with a low or medium impact.

This leaves those with high/medium impact and probability. For all of these a containment/reduction plan should be considered. This may simply be that a decision is made to ignore the risk – the impact is sufficiently low that the consequences can be lived with even if inconvenient. In other cases the plan may range from simple actions, such as checking that all staff have been trained in security procedures, through to complex sub-projects. For example, if a supplier is unable to implement a communications infrastructure then a new procurement may have to be initiated and the whole project rescheduled, in whole or in part.

The prioritization and the decision on actions to be taken will be a judgement call. These decisions can either be taken by an individual manager or a committee, whichever is appropriate for the organization concerned. What is important is that these are conscious decisions, not left to chance.

[*Note*: Do not discard the information relating to the 'low' risks – they may become more significant in the future – risk management is a continuous process. It may well be that the risk was incorrectly categorized; then at the very least it will be possible to learn from this. In addition, once a risk plan has been put in place a previously medium/high risk will often be reduced.]

Planning

In essence, planning involves deciding what action to take in order to minimize the chances of the risk happening or of its impact when it does. In the example we are looking at here the company might contact their MP, support their trade body and so on to lobby for delay/modification of any proposed health and safety legislation that would have an adverse impact. At the same time it could plan to put in place the appropriate procedures to comply with such legislation and estimate costs and how they might be mitigated when the legislation comes into force. This might be documented in a risk register (see Glossary) as below.

Risk ID	Description	Impact	Prob.	Risk plan/Owner	Date
RW1	2020 Health and Safety Act (Home workers provision) Includes new regulation concerning weekly inspections for all home workers to ensure compliance with legislation	H	M	Support CBI in lobbying for annual inspections only. Identify training plan to allow remote workers local to each other to qualify to inspect each other's premises to reduce transport/inspection cost. HR manager is owner	dd/mm/yy

Monitoring

It is necessary to review the status of risks on a regular basis once they are identified; indeed it is essential that efforts are made to identify and assess new risks as the implementation progresses. Again, with the example given, the progress and nature of the legislation and its parliamentary timetable would be watched. The risk plan could then be updated to reflect these events. This could lead to entries in the risk register similar to those below.

Risk ID	Description	Impact	Prob.	Risk plan/Owner	Date
RW1	2020 Health and Safety Act (Home workers provision) Includes new regulation concerning weekly inspections for all home workers to ensure compliance with legislation	L	H	Support CBI in lobbying for annual inspections only. Identify training plan to allow remote workers local to each other to qualify to inspect each other's premises to reduce transport/inspection cost. HR manager is owner Updated – Act modified to six monthly inspection – Impact now Low, probability High	dd/mm/yy dd/mm/yy

Sources of Risk

The table below shows the primary sources of risk for any undertaking, and as such includes areas that must be considered when implementing remote working.

External

External sources of risk can be anything from acts of terrorism and earthquakes at one end of the scale to a traffic jam making it impossible for a remote worker to get to a meeting on time.

Political

These are issues such as a change of government or political issues within an organization. For example, government legislation on health and safety for remote workers might make it impossibly expensive to implement.

Commercial

An example of commercial risk would be where a customer was financially unsound. There would be a risk of not getting paid for services and/or goods delivered if the client were to cease trading. Higher than expected communications charges for Internet access would be another example.

Technical

Technology does not meet performance requirements of remote workers. For example, emails with large file attachments might tie up the connection for so long that the worker cannot access other organization systems needed to do the job.

People

Key staff members leave or are sick at a critical point. Staff do not have the skills required to do the job in hand, they are unsuited to working remotely.

Processes

Company procedures might have so great a bureaucratic overhead that it might be too onerous to work remotely and complete the paperwork.

It might be too difficult to obtain approval to do something that is not run of the mill.

Sources of Risk for Remote Working

The following sample risks have been identified based upon both the authors' own experience and from the interviews with remote workers and employers that formed part of the research for this book. The forms used, show the risks as they might be recorded at the end of the risk identification stage. Consequently there are no identified plans/owners associated with them.

[*Note*: The impact/probabilities given, though based on the authors' experience, are not intended to be used by any specific organization, they must always be evaluated separately.]

For the Organization

Risk ID	Description	Impact	Prob.		Date
	EXTERNAL				
O0001	Travel issues – traffic congestion and/or unreliability of public transport make travel to main base/clients impractical	M	M		dd/mm/yy
O0002	Changes to tax policies, e.g. on home use of equipment	M	L		dd/mm/yy
O0003	Increases in taxation on travel may be positive or negative depending on nature of remote work	H	M		dd/mm/yy
	POLITICAL				
O0004	Health and Safety – may increase need for inspection and control of remote worker premises	H	M		dd/mm/yy

(*continued*)

Risk ID	Description	Impact	Prob.		Date
O0005	Transport policy – associated costs may be increased	M	L		dd/mm/yy
	COMMERCIAL				
O0006	Costs of remote working greater than conventional approach	H	M		dd/mm/yy
O0007	Clients unhappy about dealing with distributed workforce	H	L		dd/mm/yy
O0008	Remote working fails to deliver cost benefits	M	M		dd/mm/yy
	TECHNICAL				
O0009	Support for remotely located staff	M	M		dd/mm/yy
O0010	Time needed to implement technical solution	M	H		dd/mm/yy
O0011	Security not included in technical solution	M	H		dd/mm/yy
O0012	Impact of failures in technical infrastructure	M	H		dd/mm/yy
O0013	Data loss due to lack of rigorous back-up facilities	H	M		dd/mm/yy
O0014	Logistics support fails to deliver key equipment in a timely manner	M	M		dd/mm/yy
O0015	Software/hardware distribution and maintenance more complex	M	M		dd/mm/yy
O0016	Remote users introducing own software/data onto organization systems	H	L		dd/mm/yy
	PEOPLE				
O0018	Staff may not wish to work remotely	H	L		dd/mm/yy
O0019	Role is not suited to remote working	H	L		dd/mm/yy

(*continued*)

181

Risk ID	Description	Impact	Prob.		Date
O0020	Demotivation due to poor management and support	H	M		dd/mm/yy
O0021	Staff development more complex than for on-site staff	M	M		dd/mm/yy
O0022	Office-based staff resent perceived freedom of remote staff	M	M		dd/mm/yy
O0023	Remote staff feel they, 'are out of sight, out of mind'	H	M		dd/mm/yy
O0024	Managers do not have skills to work with remote staff	H	M		dd/mm/yy
O0025	Workers do not have correct skill set for home-based working (full or part time)	H	M		dd/mm/yy
O0026	Less effective internal communications between staff and between staff and organization	M	M		dd/mm/yy
O0027	Difficulty of measuring performance	M	M		dd/mm/yy
	PROCESS				
O0028	Time needed to develop processes	M	M		dd/mm/yy
O0029	Processes do not work effectively	H	M		dd/mm/yy
O0030	Security processes are not well enough developed to keep the required level of security needed by the organization	H	L		dd/mm/yy
O0031	Processes require too much bureaucratic overhead	M	M		dd/mm/yy
O0032	Cost of maintaining processes	M	M		dd/mm/yy
O0033	Data protection processes more complex with distributed data	H	L		dd/mm/yy
O0034	Asset management overhead	M	M		dd/mm/yy

For the Remote Worker

Risk ID	Description	Impact	Prob.		Date
	EXTERNAL				
R0001	Transport to other sites too difficult for remote worker – meetings may be difficult/expensive to attend. May take too long to reach urgent meetings	M	M		dd/mm/yy
R0002	Communications interrupted due to infrastructure failure/ virus attack preventing remote worker from accessing organization	M	M		dd/mm/yy
	POLITICAL				
R0003	Taxation/council tax issues may have adverse financial impact	M	L		dd/mm/yy
R0004	Planning and building regulations prevent conversion/affect remote working cost to worker	H	M		dd/mm/yy
	COMMERCIAL				
R0005	Costs incurred in using home as office base	M	M		dd/mm/yy
	TECHNICAL				
R0006	Remote staff finding IT equipment difficult to use reducing ability to deliver	M	M		dd/mm/yy
R0007	Support difficult to access/does not respond quickly enough so impacts ability to work	M	M		dd/mm/yy
R0008	Reliability of home equipment	M	L		dd/mm/yy
R0009	Unclear boundaries between organization and home use	M	M		dd/mm/yy
	PEOPLE				
R0010	Demotivation due to feeling isolated from	M	M		dd/mm/yy

(continued)

Risk ID	Description	Impact	Prob.		Date
	main organization/ colleagues				
R0011	Lack of visible management results in lower productivity	M	L		dd/mm/yy
R0012	Training more difficult to obtain/follow up	M	M		dd/mm/yy
R0013	Remote staff feel they 'are out of sight, out of mind'. Become demotivated and less productive – may leave the organization	M	H		dd/mm/yy
R0014	Workers do not have necessary communication skills to work remotely, so unable to do the job	M	M		dd/mm/yy
R0015	Lack of, or excessive supervision – demotivation	M	M		dd/mm/yy
R0016	Lack of interaction with colleagues	M	M		dd/mm/yy
R0017	Difficulty in working when family/other people in home environment	M	M		dd/mm/yy
R0018	Lack of space for home working	M	M		dd/mm/yy
R0019	Performance difficult to assess	M	H		dd/mm/yy
R0020	Fail to realize benefits of remote working, consequent demotivation of staff and managers	H	M		dd/mm/yy
	PROCESS				
R0021	Procedures unclear, remote worker wastes time correcting/trying to establish correct process	M	M		dd/mm/yy
R0022	Procedures do not work so remote worker unable to deliver role	H	M		dd/mm/yy
R0023	Burden of processes relating to security and maintenance of information makes remote worker unproductive	M	M		dd/mm/yy

Sample Risk Plans

The tables below, based upon the risks identified above, suggest top level actions that might be taken to reduce their impact or probability. This does not constitute a fully worked out risk plan as such. At the end of this section a few sample risks have been taken to the next stage to indicate how these risks could be more fully planned for. This should provide a good starting point for looking at potential risks to a successful remote working implementation. Ownership of the risks has been allocated to HR (Human Resources), MA (Management) or IT (Information Technology) – these have been chosen as a representative subset of what might be expected in a typical organization.

[*Note*: that the risk/impact values given were those in place before the risk plans were put in place. As part of an ongoing risk process they would be modified/removed/added to as needed.]

Organization

Risk ID	Description	Impact	Prob.	Risk plan/Owner	Date
	EXTERNAL				
O0001	Travel issues – traffic congestion and/or unreliability of public transport make travel to main base/clients impractical	M	M	Assess travel requirements as part of evaluation of viability of a role/person for remote working. Consider use of alternative technology, use of more conveniently located meeting facilities. MA	dd/mm/yy
O0002	Changes to tax policies, e.g. on home use of equipment	M	L	Monitor tax legislation and assess prior to its implementation. Lobby using trade organizations/ local MP etc. HR	dd/mm/yy
O0003	Increases in taxation on travel may be positive or negative depending on nature of remote work.	H	M	Monitor implications of any proposed changes and lobby as needed. HR	dd/mm/yy

(*continued*)

185

Risk ID	Description	Impact	Prob.	Risk plan/Owner	Date
	POLITICAL				
O0004	Health and safety – may increase need for inspection and control of remote worker premises	H	M	Identify remote worker specific health and safety costs and resource requirements and monitor trend for early warning of impact on viability of the remote working approach. HR	dd/mm/yy
O0005	Transport policy – associated costs may be increased	M	L	Encourage trade associations and lobby groups to influence policy in a favourable way. Monitor policy announcements and review costs and trends. HR	dd/mm/yy
	COMMERCIAL				
O0006	Costs of remote working greater than conventional approach	H	M	Establish criteria for remote working including increased cost versus non-tangible benefits such as flexible working and set an upper limit. Monitor, and if trend suggests limit will be breached look at options. MA	dd/mm/yy
O0007	Clients unhappy about dealing with distributed workforce	H	L	Provide central point of contact for virtual organization so that this is not visible to clients. MA	dd/mm/yy
O0008	Remote working fails to deliver cost benefits	M	M	Review case for remote working regularly to establish trends. Have a cost justification model against which to assess this. MA	dd/mm/yy
	TECHNICAL				
O0009	Support for remotely located staff	M	M	Ensure that requirements are correctly identified and that the proposed support infrastructure is capable of delivering them. HR	dd/mm/yy
O0010	Time needed to implement technical solution	M	H	Establish if a phased approach can be used for implementation, allowing those who do not need full technical facilities to start ahead of the rest. Communicate timetable to	dd/mm/yy

(continued)

Risk ID	Description	Impact	Prob.	Risk plan/Owner	Date
				staff and management. IT/MA	
O0011	Security not included in technical solution	M	H	First review any existing security policy against the added risks that come from having a remote workforce. If no policies exist, then create them for remote implementation and then consider applying them to the host organization. Measure security requirements in terms of costs and impact if they are not followed. IT	dd/mm/yy
O0012	Impact of failures in technical infrastructure	M	H	Assess likely areas of failure and determine how long failures can be tolerated before impacting remote workers. Based on this set service agreement fix times for these areas to minimize impact. Where necessary duplicate elements of infrastructure to give required levels of availability – review on-site spares holding. IT	dd/mm/yy
O0013	Data loss due to lack of rigorous back-up facilities	H	M	Provide remote staff with effective, simple, and where possible automatic, process and equipment to make back ups. Test the procedures regularly to make sure back-up data can be restored in case of failure. IT	dd/mm/yy
O0014	Logistics support fails to deliver key equipment in a timely manner	M	M	Model logistics process before setting out on large-scale implementation. If possible pilot the process to ensure that it will work. IT/MA	dd/mm/yy
O0015	Software/hardware distribution and maintenance more complex	M	M	Identify software tools and processes to automate and control software and hardware updates. Model costs of different methods to determine best practice/value for money. IT	dd/mm/yy

(*continued*)

Risk ID	Description	Impact	Prob.	Risk plan/Owner	Date
O0016	Remote users introducing own software/data onto organization systems	H	L	Combine access control software with rigorously policed procedures to minimize chances. Communicate why this is a bad idea to remote workers and why it is beneficial to them not to let this happen. IT/HR	dd/mm/yy
	PEOPLE				
O0018	Staff may not wish to work remotely	H	L	Assess individual preferences early. If it is essential that someone be home-based who does not want to, then ensure that benefits are clearly communicated. Suggest a trial period to allay fears. Ultimately if someone is unsuited to remote working then forcing them to do so will not work – look at other options. HR	dd/mm/yy
O0019	Role is not suited to remote working	H	L	Review the definition of the role to see if it can be altered to be more suitable, if not then it is a bad idea to make role remote-based and therefore unwise to continue. HR	dd/mm/yy
O0020	Demotivation due to poor management and support	H	M	Select only roles, managers and workers who are suited to remote working and provide training to ensure they all have the relevant skills. In addition make sure that support and operational procedures are well defined and tested. HR/MA	dd/mm/yy
O0021	Staff development more complex than for on site staff	M	M	Provided that training needs are identified correctly there is no more difficulty in sending remote staff on training courses than on site staff. HR	dd/mm/yy

(continued)

Risk ID	Description	Impact	Prob.	Risk plan/Owner	Date
O0022	Office-based staff resent perceived freedom of remote staff	M	M	Communicate the basis upon which roles/employees are offered remote working and demonstrate that it is fair. If it is a pilot scheme make it clear that, if successful then a wider implementation may follow. HR/MA	dd/mm/yy
O0023	Remote staff feel they 'are out of sight, out of mind'	H	M	Ensure line and HR managers have the skills needed to make sure that this is not the case, and that the remote workers are aware of this. HR	dd/mm/yy
O0024	Managers do not have skills to work with remote staff	H	M	Make evaluation of managers of remote workers part of the process for determining if a role is suitable. Develop managers who do not have the right skills. Those who are completely unsuited to managing remote staff need to be given role without remote staff. HR	dd/mm/yy
O0025	Workers do not have correct skill set for home-based working (full or part time)	H	M	Where possible develop appropriate skills to make them effective remote workers. Where not then remote working should not be implemented for those workers. HR	dd/mm/yy
O0026	Less effective internal communications between staff and between staff and organization	M	M	Promote communications using bulletin boards (on Internet/intranet), group meetings, briefings, social events and email shots. Managers should ensure they have sufficient contact time with the remote workers to communicate messages and receive feedback. HR	dd/mm/yy
O0027	Difficulty of measuring performance	M	M	Set relevant and measurable goals for both remote workers and managers. HR/MA	dd/mm/yy

(*continued*)

189

Risk ID	Description	Impact	Prob.	Risk plan/Owner	Date
	PROCESS				
O0028	Time needed to develop processes	M	M	Either choose a pilot implementation approach to prove the processes and modify as required, or review timetables against reality. MA	dd/mm/yy
O0029	Processes do not work effectively	H	M	Trial processes with a small group initially and establish practicality and performance. MA	dd/mm/yy
O0030	Security processes are not well enough developed to keep the required level of security needed by the organization	H	L	Audit security processes regularly to ensure they meet requirements. Pilot processes on a small scale to establish viability. MA	dd/mm/yy
O0031	Processes require too much bureaucratic overhead	M	M	Employ a pragmatic approach to processes and test them for usability wherever practical. If resources for developing and documenting effective process not available within the organization then consider hiring in specialists. Get feedback from those who use the processes. MA	dd/mm/yy
O0032	Cost of maintaining processes	M	M	Make processes clear and simple to maintain. Do not change processes unless there is a good reason – strong change control. MA	dd/mm/yy
O0033	Data protection processes more complex with distributed data	H	L	Assess data protection requirements and establish impact of remote working on implementing suitable safeguards. Audit processes to ensure compliance. IT/MA	dd/mm/yy
O0034	Asset management overhead	M	M	Consider issuing assets as a 'remote working' kit rather than individual items. Only track assets that are of sufficient value to require it. For example, computer systems, not mice, keyboards and the like. IT/MA	dd/mm/yy

Remote Worker

Risk ID	Description	Impact	Prob.	Contingency plan/Owner	Date
	EXTERNAL				
R0001	Transport to other sites too difficult for remote worker – meetings may be difficult/expensive to attend. May take too long to reach urgent meetings	M	M	Review transport requirements for remote worker, establish if car required/public transport options. Identify business needs versus costs and requirements for urgent meetings. This to be done before remote working agreed. HR/MA	dd/mm/yy
R0002	Communications interrupted due to infrastructure failure/ virus attack preventing remote worker from accessing organization	M	M	Ensure that infrastructure is designed to provide correct level of availability/security and has service level agreement to support this. For short term (hours) interruptions provide an off-line working facility for remote workers. IT/MA	dd/mm/yy
	POLITICAL				
R0003	Taxation/council tax issues may have adverse financial impact	M	L	Establish exact position/ liabilities for remote worker and advise accordingly. Monitor changes and advise before they impact worker. HR	dd/mm/yy
R0004	Planning and building regulations prevent conversion/ affect remote working cost to worker	H	M	Check current situation and establish that this is not a problem before starting. Monitor proposals and lobby if negative. HR	dd/mm/yy
	COMMERCIAL				
R0005	Costs incurred in using home as office base	M	M	Site survey (either by organization or potential home worker) based upon a suitable set of requirements can identify realistic costs to remote worker. HR/IT	dd/mm/yy

(*continued*)

191

Risk ID	Description	Impact	Prob.	Contingency plan/Owner	Date
TECHNICAL					
R0006	Remote staff finding IT equipment difficult to use reducing ability to deliver	M	M	Provide additional training to ensure remote workers have relevant skills. These may need to be higher than for on-site workers to reduce dependence on 'desk' visits by support staff. IT	dd/mm/yy
R0007	Support difficult to access/does not respond quickly enough so impacts ability to work	M	M	Tailor support functions to directly meet the needs of remote workers. IT	dd/mm/yy
R0008	Reliability of home equipment	M	L	Choose equipment that has a good history of reliability, avoid leading edge equipment except where essential. IT	dd/mm/yy
R0009	Unclear boundaries between organization and home use	M	M	Sponsoring organization must provide clear guidelines on use of equipment. For security reasons non-organization supplied software should be discouraged and non-business use restricted or forbidden. HR/IT	dd/mm/yy
PEOPLE					
R0010	Demotivation due to feeling isolated from main organization/ colleagues	M	M	Put in place sufficient commu-nication channels (meetings, bulletin boards, email shots, events and so forth) to mini-mize chances of isolation. HR	dd/mm/yy
R0011	Lack of visible management results in lower productivity	M	L	Ensure appropriate PR and communication channels in place. HR/MA	dd/mm/yy
R0012	Training more difficult to obtain/ follow up	M	M	Provide logistics support to coordinate training times and locations to fit needs of remote staff as far as possible. HR	dd/mm/yy
R0013	Remote staff feel they 'are out of sight, out of mind'. Become de-motivated and less productive – may leave the organization	M	H	See R0010 above – risk merged	dd/mm/yy

(continued)

Risk ID	Description	Impact	Prob.	Contingency plan/Owner	Date
R0014	Workers do not have necessary communication skills to work remotely, so unable to do the job	M	M	Assessment before selecting for remote working, provision of training where appropriate. HR	dd/mm/yy
R0015	Lack of, or excessive supervision – demotivation	M	M	Review management approach – avoid micro-managing staff but also ensure they are not just left to get on with it. HR/MA	dd/mm/yy
R0016	Lack of interaction with colleagues	M	M	See R0014 above – risk merged.	dd/mm/yy
R0017	Difficulty in working when family/other people in home environment	M	M	Provide training/mentoring. HR	dd/mm/yy
R0018	Lack of space for home working	M	M	Site audit to eliminate unsuitable locations from consideration. HR/IT	dd/mm/yy
R0019	Performance difficult to assess	M	H	Risk merged with R0020 below	dd/mm/yy
R0020	Fail to realize benefits of remote working, consequent demotivation of staff and managers	H	M	Clearly identify what these are before remote working is implemented. These may be financial or work/life balance, quality of life, productivity. However, they must be measurable. If, after a realistic period remote working fails to deliver then review role/establish why and act. HR/MA	dd/mm/yy
	PROCESS				
R0021	Procedures unclear, remote worker wastes time correcting/trying to establish correct process	M	M	Provide training in use of processes and make sure that processes are documented in a way that makes them easy to use and understand. Monitor understanding of processes and provide refresher training. HR/MA	dd/mm/yy

(*continued*)

193

Risk ID	Description	Impact	Prob.	Contingency plan/Owner	Date
R0022	Procedures do not work so remote worker unable to deliver role	H	M	Trial procedures before implementation – run a pilot scheme when practical. MA/HR	dd/mm/yy
R0023	Burden of processes relating to security and maintenance of information makes remote worker unproductive	M	M	Adopt pragmatic approach to process implementation, no unnecessary documentation/ overhead. If security issues make this impractical then review suitability of role for remote working. IT/HR	dd/mm/yy

Detailed Plan

Because it would take up more space, and not be specific to the reader's organization no detailed plan has been produced here. Specifically the detailed plan needs to add dates, timetables and ownership to the identified risks – who, what, where and when. However, to give an indication of what might be involved in such a plan, an alternative approach is described as an example.

Alternative Approach

There is another approach to risk management that can be very effective when implementing a new project or programme. It consists of developing the risk plan from the project/programme plan itself. A simple example is shown below, based upon boiling an egg and delivering it to a customer in exchange for payment. Although trivial, it serves to demonstrate the principles involved.

Step 1: Project plan

Develop project plan (or use the one that has already been produced – e.g. for implementing remote working for a department) – in this case for boiling an egg. Then identify risks associated with the resources required and the activities that will be performed in completing the project.

Resources: Saucepan, chef, electric ring, source of power, water, timer, spoon, eggcup and an egg.

Activities: Fill saucepan, place pan on electric ring, when boiling add egg (using spoon), start timer, when timer indicates 3 minutes remove

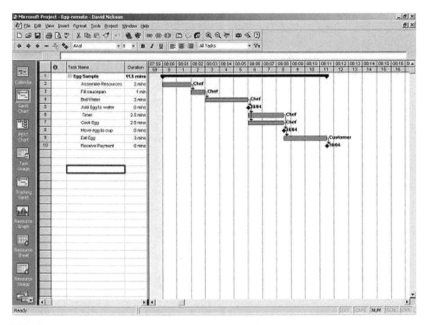

Figure 7

egg from water using spoon, place in egg cup, serve to customer, obtain payment.

This plan is shown in bar chart form in Figure 7.

Step 2: Risk assessment and plan

This is for each activity and resource.

Resources					
Risk ID	*Description*	*Impact*	*Prob.*	*Contingency plan/ Owner*	*Date*
R0001	Saucepan – not correct size or leaks	L	L	Working in kitchen – so unlikely – no plan needed, ignore	dd/mm/yy
R0002	Electric ring – not in working order	H	L	Working in kitchen – so unlikely – no plan needed, ignore	dd/mm/yy

(*continued*)

195

Risk ID	Description	Impact	Prob.	Contingency plan/ Owner	Date
R0003	Source of power – not available	H	L	Make sure electricity bill has been paid/ *Accounts Department*	dd/mm/yy
R0004	Chef – not suitably trained or available	H	M	Ensure any chef recruited can boil egg, or retrain/ *Human Resources*	dd/mm/yy
R0005	Timer – not working, or correct time range	M	L	Working in kitchen – so unlikely – no plan needed, ignore	dd/mm/yy
R0006	Spoon – not correct size	L	L	Working in kitchen – so unlikely – no plan needed, ignore	dd/mm/yy
R0007	Egg cup – not correct size	H	L	Working in kitchen – so unlikely – no plan needed, ignore	dd/mm/yy
R0008	Egg – not fresh	H	M	Arrange fresh delivery on the day/ *Procurements Department*	dd/mm/yy
R0009	Water – sufficient quantity not available	H	L	Working in kitchen – so unlikely – no plan needed, ignore	dd/mm/yy

Activities

Risk ID	Description	Impact	Prob.	Contingency plan/ Owner	Date
A0001	Assemble resources – resources not available so unable to proceed	H	L	Working in kitchen – so unlikely – no plan needed, ignore	dd/mm/yy

(*continued*)

Risk ID	Description	Impact	Prob.	Contingency plan/ Owner	Date
A0002	Fill saucepan – handle breaks	L	L	No action required as unlikely	dd/mm/yy
A0003	Boil water – risk of scalding if spilt	H	M	Apply safety procedure (tested beforehand) to ensure low risk/*Chef*	dd/mm/yy
A0004	Timer – failed to wind up first so did not start	M	M	Ensure chef has watch as standby facility/ *Chef*	dd/mm/yy
A0005	Cook egg – egg cracks making unattractive to customer	H	M	Have back-up stock of eggs as standby – one dozen/ *Procurement Department.*	dd/mm/yy
A0006	Move egg – egg dropped in transit	H	M	Have back-up stock and place egg cup next to saucepan to minimize travel requirement/ *Procurement and Chef*	dd/mm/yy
A0007	Eat egg – customer allergic	H	L	If necessary get customer to sign disclaimer against allergy	dd/mm/yy
A0008	Receive payment – customer has no money	H	L	Check credit rating of client prior to starting/*Accounts*	dd/mm/yy

The benefit of this approach is that both the risk plan and the project plan are clearly related to one another and that any change to the plan is the cue to reassessment of the related risks. The downside is that it can result in a significant bureaucratic overhead, and because the risks are based upon the plan it can lead to higher level risks being ignored. It is task- rather than strategy-oriented. The authors leave it to the judgement, and practices, of the organization involved as to its adoption or not.

A large American IT organization implemented a form of remote working in the 1980s. This included the setting up of a 'hot desking' centre (see Glossary) for the employees to visit when they needed to get on the corporate network; technology at the time was too expensive for more than basic home email. Because the goal was to keep used floor space to a minimum the hot desk centre had more than a passing resemblance to pig pens. There was just enough space to sit at the PC keyboard in a small partitioned closet. There wasn't even enough room to hang a coat, put work down to read and so on. Consequently the remote workers felt that when they visited the main organization they were treated as worthless. The morale of these staff was low and performance and productivity both suffered. The lesson to be learnt from this is that remote workers must be treated as equals when they do visit the main office bases. Drop-in, or hot desk facilities have to be as good as for on-site staff. After all, the remote worker is likely to be there for several hours, or even a day at a time. A permanent desk is not an option but enough space for the individuals to work normally and have their own territory is. The risk register that is presented in this chapter should have captured this problem.

Summary

The benefits of risk management have been well established in both the public and private sectors. For anything that involves significant organizational change, as the implementation of remote working does, assessing the risks and taking appropriate action to contain them is highly recommended. The sample risks and plans given here are a starting point for any organization considering embarking upon remote working and will save considerable time compared to developing them from scratch. Time spent in risk management will significantly improve the chances of a successful outcome.

Appendix A: Example Work Practices

This example is based upon one kindly provided by the Silicon Graphics (UK) Human Resources Department and the authors acknowledge their copyright in this information. You may use it as the basis for your own work practices but may not use it verbatim without the permission of Silicon Graphics (UK).

Home-Working Policy

Definition

If you spend more than 80% of your normal working week working at or from home, or if you travel on average less than 1 day per week to the office, and do not have a desk at the office, you are a home worker. You should have a contract of employment or a letter confirming home as your place of work.

If you occasionally work from home, either voluntarily or because circumstances make it impossible for you to travel, this does *not* make you a home worker.

[*Note: This policy relates to home workers only.*]

Home working may not be appropriate for all employees, because of job requirements, the particular employee's skill-set, or lack of access to an appropriate environment. It is the manager and HR who ultimately determine if this arrangement is appropriate and meets business objectives.

[*Note. Home working is not a right of employment at SGI.*]

You need to consider the following before making the decision to work at home:

1. Is your home suited to home working?

- ☐ Do you have a suitable room in your home to convert to an office where you can work effectively?
- ☐ Is your home free of any distractions that could affect your work? For example, if you have children, do you have appropriate child-care arrangements to ensure they cannot interfere with your work?

2. Do you feel you are suited to home working?

- ☐ Do you have the right motivation to work remotely?
- ☐ Do you have good time management, planning and organizing skills?
- ☐ Are you self-disciplined?
- ☐ Will you be getting everything you need from your job being based at home? What about the social aspects, i.e. being on your own all day, every day or most days?

3. Is your job suitable for home working?

- ☐ Does it involve 'thinking tasks' such as writing, research, programming or analysing?
- ☐ Can you and your manager measure productivity in terms of the number of projects or objectives completed?
- ☐ Can you work without constant access to corporate office off-line files or equipment?
- ☐ Can you work without daily face-to-face contact with other employees?
- ☐ Does your role require little supervision?
- ☐ Can you work outside the office without this having an adverse effect on the team you work with?
- ☐ Can you do your work without having to visit the office regularly?

Your manager will help you to make this assessment.

If you are able to answer all the above questions positively and your manager and HR are in agreement, you will need to do the following before commencing home working:

- ■ Contact your home contents insurance company to inform them that you will be converting a room to an office and working from home on a regular basis. There is no need to cover any office equipment belonging to the company (as this will be covered by the company's own insurance policy).

- Contact your mortgage company/landlord and tell them you will now work from home (in case of any additional charges – we will meet these if applicable).
- Contact your local council planning authority to let them know your home has altered status (in case of any additional charges – we will meet these if applicable).
- Ensure you have itemized billing on your telephone line; possibly consider a separate line and number to ensure that costs can be claimed easily.
- Ensure you have adequate power and lighting in your chosen designated work area to handle the equipment that will be installed.

The company as your employer will

- Provide a written contract of employment stating your home is your place of work and establishing your core hours of working.
- Inspect your home to ensure that it is suitable for home working and compliant with all health and safety legislation.
- Provide and install all the suitable equipment required in your preferred location and check that any equipment you use meets health and safety standards – see below.
- Insure this equipment against loss or damage (we will meet any additional costs incurred as a result of any increase in your home insurance premium because you are home working).
- Forward your post to your home address.

[*Note*: Your manager will ensure that you have regular contact with him/her and your colleagues as well as any information you require for your job.]

The company may require your work schedule to be altered, from time to time, due to training sessions, meetings, etc. You are expected to spend time in your primary business location as necessary to fulfil the requirements of your job and as directed by your manager.

If you wish to change your work location from home back to the company office, you would need to give sufficient notice (at least one month). The company reserves the right to refuse any such request on the grounds that it may not suit the company's business purpose and may not be practical at that particular time. The company reserves the right to change your place of work back to a company office location subject to the company's business needs, but will give you at least one month's notice of its intention to do so.

Equipment

Your manager will agree what equipment is appropriate, depending on your job. You may be provided with the following equipment as appropriate at SGI's cost:

- Desk and chair (if you wish to use your own it must be suitable and comply with health and safety requirements).
- Lockable filing cabinet.
- Computer.
- Printer.
- Fax machine (if needed).
- Telephone and answerphone.
- Second dedicated business line.
- ISDN line for permanent connection to SGI network.

We will meet the costs of any minor modifications as well as making good any disturbance to home décor when equipment is installed and removed.

Health and safety

You are responsible for your own health and safety and the health and safety of others at your place of work.

If you have an accident at work you should report it using the relevant form. This is available from HR.

SGI will ensure you have the appropriate training to handle any equipment provided. The Health and Safety Officer or appointed person will regularly inspect your property to ensure everything is running smoothly. Electrical appliances will be tested as appropriate under health and safety regulations.

Expenses

SGI will reimburse you for agreed and reasonable expenses which are incurred as a result of working at home (as defined under the Expenses policy, e.g. telephone bills).

We will pay you business mileage expense from your home as your permanent place of work. Visits to the office count for business miles. See mileage rates in Expenses section of the HR Website.

You will receive £15 per month as a home-working allowance, provided you satisfy all our criteria. (You will only be entitled to an allowance if you genuinely spend at least 60% of your time actually working from your home office.) This will be paid monthly with your normal salary via payroll and taxed in the usual manner, and is to cover costs such as heating, lighting and water.

In exceptional circumstances, if you feel that your costs exceed the amount of this allowance, you should make a claim through your immediate manager who would need to authorize any additional expense.

Your responsibilities

- Ensure the working environment you create will be safe (guidance and training will be given upon inspection).
- Take reasonable care to safeguard company property.
- If loss or theft of SGI property does occur, you are expected to report the incident immediately to the police and SGI Facilities department.
- Under the Data Protection Act you are expected to keep secure any company information/data held on your premises at all times.
- Ensure you follow the Display Screen Equipment guidelines so that your computer is set up correctly (after installation and use).
- Ensure that you sit properly in your chair. SGI will provide footrests, wrist rests, screen covers as necessary to ensure your comfort and protection from injury.
- You should take regular breaks from your work.
- You will not conduct SGI business meetings with third parties at the home-office site.

- Return any equipment should you cease to be a home worker or cease to be employed by SGI, see 'Leaving SGI' section of HR Website.

SGI reserves the right to amend, suspend or withdraw this policy, without notice, at its discretion.

Issue: July 2001

Appendix B: Plain English Remote Working Policy

The document below has been based upon a number of policies that the authors have been shown, and has been turned into as plain language as possible. In practice, because they have contractual significance, these policies are typically worded using legal terminology. The authors humbly suggest that where this is the case a plain English version is made available too.

- The organization may need to change the terms and conditions that apply to you for remote working. The organization has the right to cancel remote working at any time and base you at an office. However, you will be consulted about this and given at least a month's notice of the change.
- So that the organization can operate efficiently we will need to give your home address and a business phone number to co-workers and to customers.
- Your personnel records will note that you are home-based and that address will be used for business correspondence.
- It is up to you to make sure that you have insurance that allows you to use part of your home as an office and that you have enough cover.
- You must make sure there is enough space to work in your home and that it is secure enough to keep equipment and information safe. If in doubt ask personnel to advise you.
- If things change and you move home or no longer have enough space for the home office then you must let the organization know, you must do this at least a month before the change happens, unless there are special reasons (for example a fire) that make this impossible.
- All the terms and conditions of your original contract, for example concerning confidential information, company property and the like still apply. Remote workers have to follow the same rules as office-based

workers. You will have the same contract of employment as before, together with any extra conditions specific to remote working.

- The same rules for use of the organization's telephones, internet and email systems apply to home use just as they do at the office.

- You may not install non-organization-supplied software on the home-based computer or allow the equipment to be used by anyone who does not belong to the organization. Your family can't use it for playing games.

- Because you are no longer on organization premises it may be necessary for other organization employees to visit your remote base. There are a number of reasons for this, including health and safety inspections, audits, repairing and replacing equipment and so on. Please make sure that your home office meets with the organization's health and safety code (ask personnel for a copy) to safeguard yourself and other organization staff who may visit.

- For insurance reasons do not hold meetings with clients or any non-organization staff at your remote base.

- If and when remote-based equipment fails you have to notify the support desk straight away. The same applies for any health and safety issues or accidents. This is just the same as for office-based workers except that the notification is done by phone or email.

- You can claim travel expenses from your remote (home) base in the same way, and under the same rules, as you did from the office base. Personnel will explain what you need to tell the Inland Revenue to keep your returns correct.

- When you stop being a home worker, or if you leave the organization, then you will have to give back anything that belongs to the organization. If asked, you will have to allow a company representative inspect the home office to make sure that this has been done.

Appendix C: Site Survey Form

This is a template for a site survey form to be used when assessing a remote worker's home base for suitability.

Date: Visit/Revisit	Name and Address:	
Item	Detail	Yes/No
Location	Is it within 2 hours of an organization office? Heat, light and power available?	
Access	Vehicle access? Doorways/steps acceptable for deliveries? Disabled access (if relevant)?	
Communications	Phone line available? Broadband available? ISDN available? Public transport within acceptable range? Premises suitable for LAN/WLAN installation?	
Health and safety	Does proposed office/working area meet H&S requirements? Does workstation installation meet requirement? Pets and relatives – is their access controlled to safeguard equipment/them?	
Security	Are premises physically secure? Alarm required? Alarm fitted?	
Legal restrictions	Is property freehold? If leasehold does lease permit business use? Are there any restrictions on use of premises that prevent home working?	
Insurance	Existing cover adequate? Quotation required?	
Other	Additional comments/further action needed	
Completed by	Name:	
Recommendation *Delete as appropriate*	Yes Yes, Further action/revisit required No	

Glossary

Although every attempt has been made to explain any special terms as they are introduced in the book, readers may find this Glossary of acronyms and abbreviations useful.

BCS	British Computer Society
Broadband	Higher speed connection for data and telephone communication using existing telephone exchange connections
Bit	Binary digit
Byte	8 bits
CIPD	Chartered Institute of Personnel and Development
COSHH	Care of Substances Hazardous to Health
Dial up	Connection to the Internet/email using a modem over a conventional telephone line
Email	Electronic mail
Extranet	External Internet
H&S	Health and safety (within the terms of the Health and Safety at Work Act)
Hot desking	Practice where staff members have no permanent desk but have access to facilities when on company premises via a pool of shared desks
HR	Human resources (department), also known as Personnel
Internet	Public access information distribution system, often used to support email and WWW transmission
Intranet	Internet-like information distribution system only accessible from within an organization

ISDN	Independent Switched Data Network. A faster alternative to a dial up connection offering simultaneous data and telephone connection over a dedicated connection
ISP	Internet Service Provider
IT	Information technology
LAN	Local area network
MODEM	MOdulator/DEModulator – a communications device for sending digital information over an analogue communications connection such as a telephone line
MS	Microsoft – software supplier
PC	Personal computer – implies systems derived from original IBM design
PRINCE	A project management system (Projects in a Controlled Environment) that includes risk and change control
Risk management	Process for recording, assessing and planning to minimize the risks that could affect a project
SLA	Service level agreement
WBS	Work package Breakdown Structure – term used in project management for showing how work is split up within a project
Website	Site on the Internet/WWW presenting information in page format. May include words, pictures, audio, video and so on
WLAN	Wireless local area network
WP	Word processor. Text manipulation application – vital for producing bid documents etc. A component of all office suites
WWW	World Wide Web – Internet page-based sources of information

Bibliography and Sources

The books listed here are recommended for further reading or for access to some of the more significant source material used by the authors. For reasons of space and practicality, not every newspaper or magazine article, website and publication that we looked at has been included.

Books

Business Communications, David Nickson and Suzy Siddons, Butterworth-Heinemann, ISBN 0-7506-2572-4

The Complete Time Management System, Christian H. Godefroy and John Clark Piatkus, ISBN 0-86188-990-8

Developing Your People, Suzy Siddons, CIPD, ISBN 0-85292-889-0

Effective Time Management: How to Save Time and Spend it Wisely, John Adair, Pan Books, ISBN 0-330-30229-9

Financial Times Handbook of Management, Pitman, ISBN 0-273-60694-8

Handbook of Management Skills, Industrial Society Press, ISBN 0-85290-903-9

Management, Richard L. Daft, Dryden Press, ISBN 0-03-047097-8

Management Teams, R. Meredith Belbin, Butterworth-Heinemann, ISBN 0-7506-0253-8

Managing International Teams, Nicola Phillips, Pitman, ISBN 0-273-03804-4

Managing Projects, David Nickson and Suzy Siddons, Butterworth-Heinemann, ISBN 0-7506-3471-5

Mentoring and Diversity, David Clutterbuck and Belle Rose Ragins, Butterworth-Heinemann, ISBN 0-7506-4836-8

The Plain English Guide, Oxford University Press, ISBN 0-19-860049

Presentation Skills, Suzy Siddons, CIPD, ISBN 0-85292-810-5

Psychology in Business, Eugene F. McKenna, LEA, ISBN 0-86377-042-8

The RAF Pocket Book 1937 (AP 1081) (out of print)

Periodicals

BCS *Computer Bulletin*, articles on technology, teleworking and management

Computer Weekly, www.ComputerWeekly.com, articles on teleworking, technology etc.

The Financial Times, various articles

Independent, various articles

SC Magazine, www.scmagazine.com, various articles on remote working, security and technology

The Times, various articles

XPERT HR, http://holland.butterworths.co.uk (subscription only service), HR articles on remote working

Websites

www.bcs.org – technology, teleworking and management

www.ogc.gov.uk – Office of Government Commerce – source of useful information

www.scmagazine.com – IT security

www.sustel.org SUSTEL IST-2001-33228 Sustainable Telework – assessing and optimizing the ecological and social benefits of teleworking

www.sustel.org TELEWORKING AT BT – the economic, environmental and social impacts of its work*about* scheme, report on survey results 14/10/2002, Dr Peter Hopkinson, Professor Peter James and Takao Maruyama

www.UK-HRD.com – e-forum for HR/People

Organizations

CIPD (Chartered Institute of Personnel and Development)

The Industrial Society

OGC (Office of Government Commerce)

Silicon Graphics UK HR Department

Index

Acquired Need Theory, 48
Action plan, 65, 69
Appraisal, 10, 27, 53, 58, 59, 61, 62, 63, 64, 66, 67, 68, 69, 70, 131
Assumptions, 36, 63

Benefits, 2, 25, 26, 29, 117, 150, 163, 198
Broadband, 41, 97, 98, 99, 100, 106

Career development, 27, 42, 131
Central Control, 113
Change, 12, 176, 179
Children, 9, 40, 43, 102, 146, 163, 164, 165, 166, 167, 168, 169, 171
Clarifying, 123
Communication, 10, 17, 26, 27, 35, 36, 37, 55, 63, 84, 97, 98, 101, 102, 103, 104, 118, 131, 132, 133, 172, 184, 192, 193
Computers, 25, 34, 112, 117, 141
Consumables, 79
Contingency planning, 72
Continuity, 115, 141, 161
Contract of employment, 18, 41
Control, 9, 28, 35, 49, 54, 59, 65, 71, 72, 75, 96, 110, 111, 113, 117, 126, 129, 142, 163, 170, 180, 186, 187, 188, 190
Conversions, 148, 155, 157
Corporate training needs, 75
COSHH, 156, 157, 159, 162
Costs, 2, 8, 11, 16, 25, 26, 27, 29, 41, 42, 48, 52, 79, 81, 84, 85, 90, 98, 100, 101, 103, 107, 117, 118, 138, 152, 154, 160, 177, 181, 186, 187, 191

Crises, 128
Customer satisfaction, 74

Decision making, 32, 36, 121, 134
Delegation, 10, 17, 27
Demotivation, 70
Dependants, 163, 166, 169
Development, 27, 28, 42, 43, 45, 46, 58, 65, 66, 67, 69, 75, 76, 77, 78, 82, 84, 160, 182, 188
DTI, 2

Environment, 4, 6, 8, 9, 10, 11, 18, 24, 52, 72, 87, 105, 117, 135, 137, 138, 139, 142, 145, 146, 152, 161, 162, 163, 170, 171, 173, 184, 193
Expectancy Theory, 46, 47

Facilitation, 33
Fax, 41, 106
Feedback, 36, 37, 43, 44, 45, 46, 53, 54, 55, 57, 69, 70, 74, 77, 134
Filing, 41, 122, 126, 127, 138, 144, 148, 157
Financial reporting, 80
Flexibility, 2, 25, 63, 65, 71, 164, 172
Furniture, 19, 39, 85, 88, 138, 140, 144, 145, 148

Goals, 12, 45, 60, 61, 62, 64, 65, 66, 189

Health and safety, 3, 13, 14, 18, 22, 24, 29, 41, 80, 134, 138, 140, 141, 145, 146, 155, 161, 176, 186
Home offices, 143
Hot desking, 198

Illness, 165
Implementation, 7, 10, 12, 13, 22, 26,
    80, 81, 85, 89, 90, 100, 110, 116, 159,
    160, 175, 176, 178, 185, 198
In-house transport, 84, 85
Induction, 89, 144, 158, 159, 162
Information technology, 28, 33, 34, 81,
    93, 115, 185
Infrastructure, 2, 8, 24, 39, 81, 84, 85, 87,
    90, 161, 177, 181, 183, 186, 187, 191
Installation, 3, 8, 19, 96, 99, 100, 105,
    107, 110, 154
Insurance, 18, 40, 41, 107, 140, 151,
    154, 155
Interviews, 45, 64
Intranet, 97, 111, 189
ISDN, 41, 98, 99

Job description, 59, 60, 75

Kittens, 171, 172

Landlord, 40, 41, 149, 153, 154
Logistics, 9, 12, 18, 24, 40, 41, 70, 80,
    81, 82, 83, 85, 86, 88, 89, 90, 91, 105,
    181, 192

McCambridge Associates, 39
Maintenance, 4, 9, 22, 80, 82, 83, 86,
    89, 91, 93, 96, 105, 107, 108, 109,
    110, 112, 117, 122, 137, 143, 146,
    181, 184, 187, 194
Manufacturing, 22, 60, 74
Maslow, 38, 45
Meetings, 9, 17, 25, 43, 44, 46, 55, 56,
    74, 76, 80, 87, 123, 124, 125, 138,
    147, 155, 158, 183, 189, 191, 192
Mentoring, 43, 51, 52, 193
Micromanagement, 32, 33, 46
Mobile Phones, 101
Monitoring, 8, 12, 19, 89, 157, 164, 175
Morale, 25, 26, 78
Motivation, 10, 26, 27, 33, 37, 46, 47,
    48, 49, 77, 121, 129, 182, 183, 184,
    188, 192, 193

Objectives, 35, 50, 51, 58, 59, 63, 66,
    68, 74
Office expenses, 29
Operational Considerations, 5
Opportunities, 42, 45, 46, 62, 76, 77, 131
Organizational change, 198
Organizational skills, 11
Organizing, 31, 67

Pagers, 104
Paperwork, 12, 88, 126, 128, 129, 179
Partners, 168
Payroll, 18
Personal skills, 26, 27, 121
Pets, 18, 146, 163, 171, 172, 173
Planning, 9, 31, 49, 50, 51, 66, 68, 72,
    74, 75, 79, 87, 175, 177
Policies, 11, 13, 14, 16, 18, 19, 37, 89,
    116, 158, 161, 170
Postal services, 83
Power and light, 41
PRINCE 2, 175
Prioritizing, 122, 124, 129
Privacy, 169
Problems, 4, 10, 36, 43, 44, 45, 58, 59,
    63, 73, 74, 79, 83, 86, 87, 104,
    108, 128, 131, 134, 147, 159, 164,
    166, 171
Procedures, 11, 89, 110, 184, 193, 194
Processes, 9, 11, 12, 16, 18, 19, 28, 32,
    39, 40, 81, 87, 89, 90, 91, 109, 111,
    114, 119, 156, 160, 182, 184, 187,
    190, 193, 194
Productivity, 2, 10, 35, 78, 130, 172,
    184, 192, 193, 198
Progress reporting, 37
Progression, 42, 43, 58
Projects, 7, 10, 15, 25, 43, 44, 51, 61,
    73, 76, 129, 152, 177, 194, 197
Promotion, 58, 76
Puppies, 171, 172
Purchasing, 86, 126

Quality checkpoints, 74

Redundancies, 43
Relatives, 163, 166, 169, 172
Reporting, 11, 37, 71, 73, 89, 124
Resources, 8, 47, 50, 52, 54, 58, 59, 72, 73, 75, 77, 111, 134, 160, 190, 194, 196
Responsibilities, 6, 37, 58
Risk, 9, 10, 11, 13, 14, 72, 73, 74, 83, 113, 114, 115, 155, 156, 160, 170, 172, 175, 176, 177, 178, 179, 180, 185, 192, 193, 194, 197, 198
Role, 11, 12, 13, 16, 17, 21, 22, 24, 25, 26, 27, 28, 29, 33, 35, 44, 59, 82, 85, 142, 143, 158, 181, 184, 185, 188, 189, 193, 194
Rules, 5, 28, 54, 72, 111, 128, 132, 134, 155, 158, 165, 167, 168, 169

Safety, 118
Salary planning, 58
Security, 8, 9, 18, 22, 23, 77, 107, 110, 112, 113, 119, 141, 160, 170, 181, 182, 187, 190
Self development, 43
Self organization, 121
Service levels, 191

Social aspects, 35
Specifications, 51, 74, 93, 128
Supervision, 10, 22, 33, 35, 184, 193
Support, 9, 12, 16, 17, 18, 27, 95, 105, 108, 178, 181, 183, 186, 192

Targets, 32, 116
Tax issues, 151, 183, 191
Technical support, 9, 105
Telephones, 143
Teleworking, 1, 166
Terms and conditions, 12
Time management, 10, 11, 17, 33, 34, 55, 56, 121, 122, 165, 168
Tracking inventory, 85
Training, 3, 27, 50, 51, 62, 77, 104, 158, 162, 184, 192
Travelling, 2, 3, 23, 25, 29, 123, 124
Trust, 10, 26, 31, 32, 47, 49, 63

Vroom, 46

Work–life balance, 24, 25, 26, 29, 163
Written communication, 133

Xansa, 40